Journeys of the Children of Israel

First published by
Vallentine, Mitchell & Co. Ltd.,
18 Cursitor Street, London E.C.4.

© the Jewish National Fund, 1966

2nd edition (revised) 1967

Printed in Great Britain by
Thomas Nelson (Printers) Ltd, London and Edinburgh

A Guide to the Study of the Bible

Journeys of the Children of Israel

by Moshe Davis and Isaac Levy

design by Hans Schwarz
based on original illustrations by the late Walter Herz

London
Vallentine, Mitchell
in association with the Jewish National Fund

Contents

A well defined map is an essential aid to the study of the Bible. Most of the existing Biblical atlases contain such an abundance, if not excess, of material, that they impede rather than assist the average student. A distinctive character of the present production is the concentration of attention on periods and events in Biblical history. Each map marks only those places mentioned in a particular narrative, thereby assisting in the identification of the relevant geographical locations.

The task of accurate identification of Biblical place-names is, however, fraught with difficulty and, rather than indulge in guess work, certain places mentioned in the Biblical texts have, of necessity, been omitted. The Hebrew spelling of place-names throughout these maps generally follows the Biblical text in the chapters concerned. Biblical references are according to the Jewish division of chapters. All differences from it in the Authorised (King James) Version are marked by the letters AV followed by the appropriate reference.

These maps are based upon the original Hebrew text and, as far as possible, each narrative is treated separately. Thus the maps are subordinated to the text. Little has been added by way of commentary, preferring to utilise the word of the Bible as its own commentary.

Greater emphasis has been placed upon the period of the Kings, as the earlier periods, particularly of the Pentateuch, are more familiar to most readers and the material relating to them is more readily available.

An attempt has been made to classify events, especially those dealing with wars, battles and the campaigns of national leaders. These narratives, as portrayed in the Bible, often create confusion in the mind of the student, who may be tempted to regard the period of Kings, for example, as one continuous and somewhat haphazard struggle. In fact, all these narratives reflect well-planned campaigns which can be followed and studied as easily as battles of recent times.

This book was originally produced in loose-leaf form, and the grateful thanks of the authors are due to many teachers and educationists who expressed their interest in the original production and encouraged the promotion of this project. Much of their advice and many of their suggestions have been incorporated in this edition.

Tribute is paid to the late Mr. Walter Herz, the artist responsible for the original artwork.

The
Holy Land
and its
Neighbours

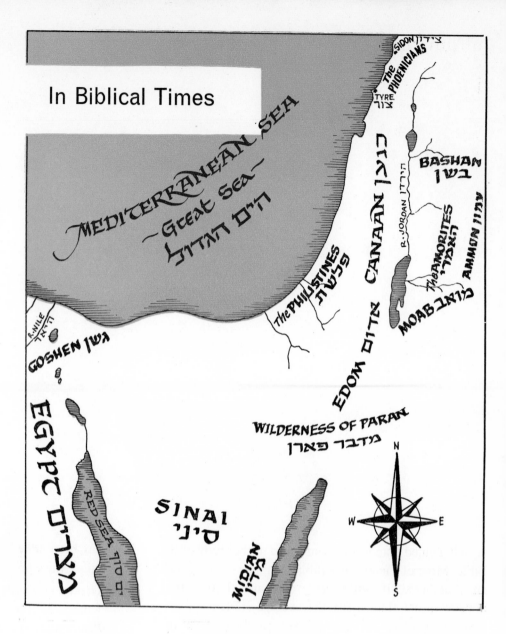

In Biblical Times

Whilst the Biblical narrative is mainly concerned with the story of the Hebrews, i.e. the descendants of Abraham, it also impinges on the inhabitants of the surrounding countries.

To the south-west of the Land of Canaan lay Egypt. Egypt first features as early as the time of Abraham who "went down into Egypt". (Gen. 12 (10).) From the story of Joseph and the Exodus we learn that Egypt was a mighty power, with a highly developed civilisation. Militarily, Egypt became more closely involved with Israel from the time of Solomon onwards, and especially in the days of Josiah and Jehoahaz of Judah.

In close proximity to the territory occupied by Israel lay the land of the Philistines (from whom is derived the name "Palestine"), whose warriors frequently terrorised the inhabitants of Canaan. Throughout the period of the Judges and the early Kings, more or less continuous war was waged between the Philistines and the Israelites.

To the south and to the east were the lands of the Edomites, the Moabites and the Amorites. These warring, nomadic tribes fought against Israel from the time of its entry into the land. As a result, the borders were constantly changing.

Only to the north, in Phoenicia, lay a friendly power. In the time of Solomon, materials for the Temple were brought to Jerusalem from Phoenicia. An alliance was entered into between Solomon and Hiram, king of Tyre, who was even given a section of Jewish territory (Cabul) within Solomon's domain.

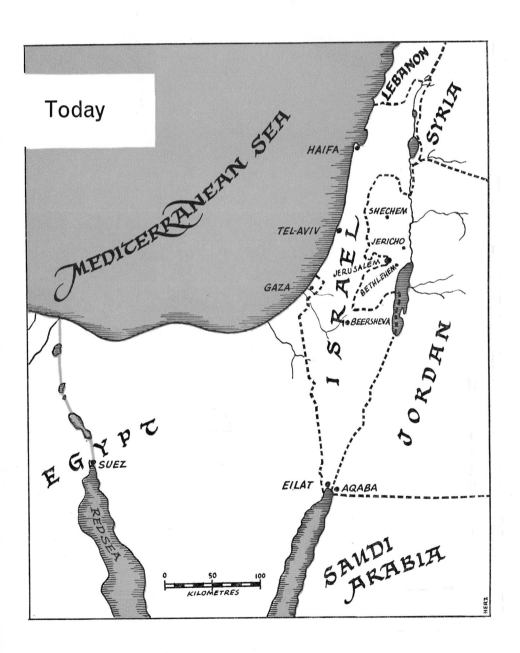

Today

MEDITERRANEAN SEA

LEBANON

SYRIA

HAIFA

TEL-AVIV

ISRAEL

SHECHEM

JERICHO

JERUSALEM

BETHLEHEM

GAZA

BEERSHEVA

JORDAN

EGYPT

SUEZ

RED SEA

EILAT

AQABA

SAUDI ARABIA

0   50   100

KILOMETRES

HERZ

The area of the Middle East today which corresponds to the Holy Land of Biblical times is, broadly speaking, occupied by the State of Israel and the Kingdom of Jordan.

The city of Jerusalem is actually divided between the two states, but all the Old City, including the reputed site of the Temple, is in the Jordanian section. Within Israeli territory lies Mt. Zion, whereon is reputed to lie the Tomb of David, and the Valley of Hinnom. Mt. Zion was included within the walls of Jerusalem in ancient times and it marked the limit of the Upper City.

Of the remaining places of Biblical note, Nazareth and the Lake of Galilee are in Israel, whilst Bethlehem, Hebron and Shechem (Nablus) are in Jordan. The River Jordan flows through both countries.

The Gaza Strip, at present occupied by Egypt, roughly corresponds to the ancient land of the Philistines and derives its name from one of the five famous ancient Philistine cities of that name. The remaining four Philistine cities: Ashkelon, Gath, Ashdod and Ekron, are associated with sites now within the area of the State of Israel.

The present shape of the State of Israel does not therefore correspond to the ancient Jewish State or to the kingdoms of Judah and Israel.

The
Holy Land
its Regions

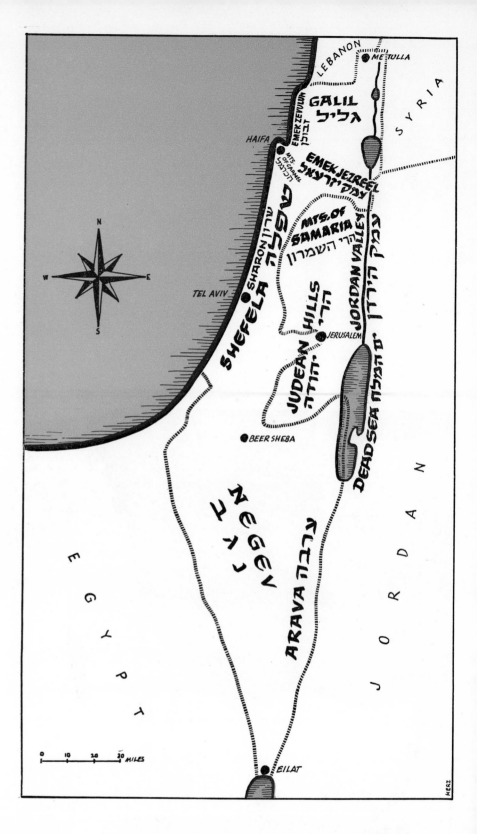

The Holy Land is divided into four main regions: the Coastal Plain, the Central Hills, the Jordan Depression and Trans-Jordan.

The southern portion of the Coastal Plain is termed the "Shefela" (Hebrew: "Lowland") and the northern section, beyond the River Yarkon, is named the "Sharon" (Hebrew: "Plain"). Both of these names are found in the Bible.

Continuing northwards along the coast, the Carmel range of hills interrupts the Coastal Plain and comes right through to the sea. In the far north is the Valley of Zebulun.

The Central Hills start in the south as the Negev range, continue as the Judean Hills and Mountains of Samaria and, in the far north, become Lower and Upper Galilee.

From east to west, dividing the Mountains of Samaria from the Hills of Galilee, runs the Valley of Jezreel (Esdraelon).

The Jordan Depression provides an unusual physical feature. Just north of Lake Kinneret (also known as Lake Galilee and Lake Tiberias), the River Jordan falls below sea level and continues its flow until it finally enters the Dead Sea and reaching to the Gulf of Eilat (Gulf of Aqaba) this Rift Valley continues under the Biblical name "Arava".

To the far east is the Trans-Jordan Plateau.

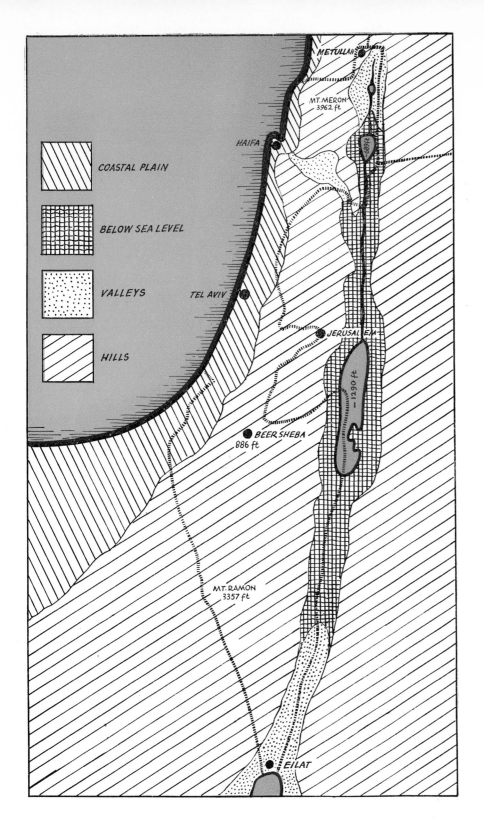

COASTAL PLAIN

BELOW SEA LEVEL

VALLEYS

HILLS

METULLAH

MT. MERON
3,962 ft

HAIFA

-689 ft

TEL AVIV

JERUSALEM

-1,290 ft

BEER SHEBA
886 ft

MT. RAMON
3357 ft

EILAT

Relief

For a small country, the Holy Land has a wide diversity of physical features. The highest point of the country is Mt. Meron, 3,962 ft., whilst the Jordan Valley depression is nearly 1,300 ft. below sea level at the Dead Sea. This is the lowest surface on earth.

The history of the country in Biblical times was continually affected by the geography of the country. Thus, for example, Joshua's first conquest was of the central hill country, and the Israelites experienced considerable difficulty in control-ling large areas of the lowlands, e.g. the land of the Philistines. In time of battle, the Israelites preferred to fight in the hill country where enemy chariots were at a disadvantage.

The Valley of Jezreel, traversing the country, was one of the main routes, both for trade and for invading armies.

It should be borne in mind that the widely ranging physical features of the country are contained within an area less than 300 miles from north to south and 100 miles east to west.

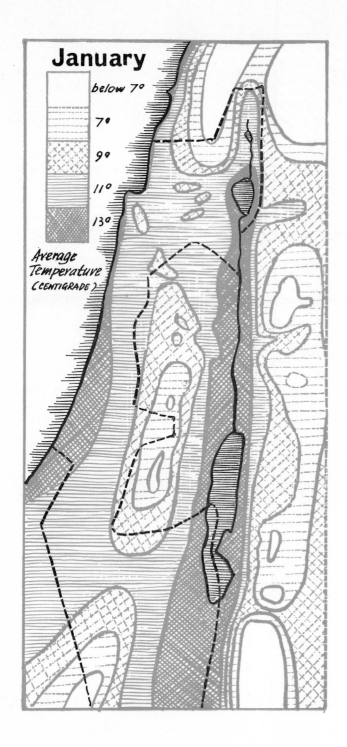

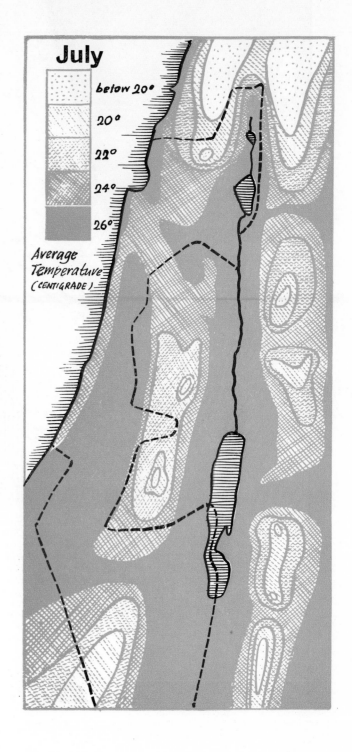

Winter

The rainy period is from October ("the former rain") to April. The heaviest rainfall is between December and February ("the latter rain"). Temperatures can be quite low and, in the hilly country, there is occasional snow.

Summer

The summer is dry and temperatures during the day can be very high. During the summer season, the "Hamsin" (a hot, dry, easterly wind) sometimes blows and causes discomfort.

The Natural Resources of the Holy Land fall into four main categories:

(a) Chemicals are found in areas of the Negev and especially in the Dead Sea. These represent the most valuable of the resources.

(b) Building materials and clays are found, especially in the north.

(c) Metals (iron and copper) are particularly associated with the south. Timna, near Eilath, is the reputed site of King Solomon's mines.

(d) Most important among the remaining resources is oil. At present this is only found in small quantities near the area of the Gaza Strip. There is no direct mention in the Bible of the presence of mineral oil.

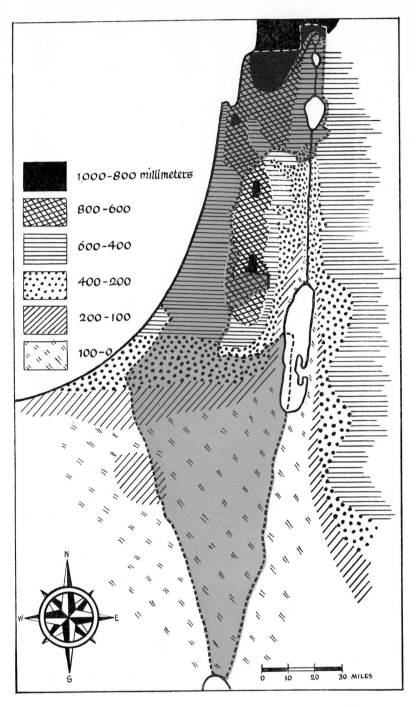

Israel has two seasons: winter (cool and rainy) and summer (hot and dry).

Temperatures vary greatly between the north and south of the country, between the hills and the low-lying ground and between night and day. When considering the average temperatures, it is necessary to take into consideration that the day temperature can be considerably higher and the night temperature much lower.

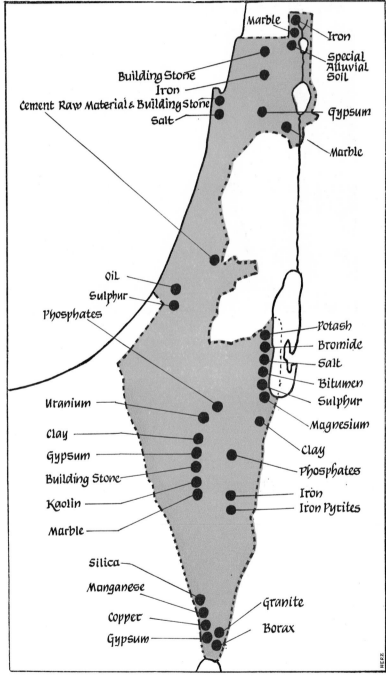

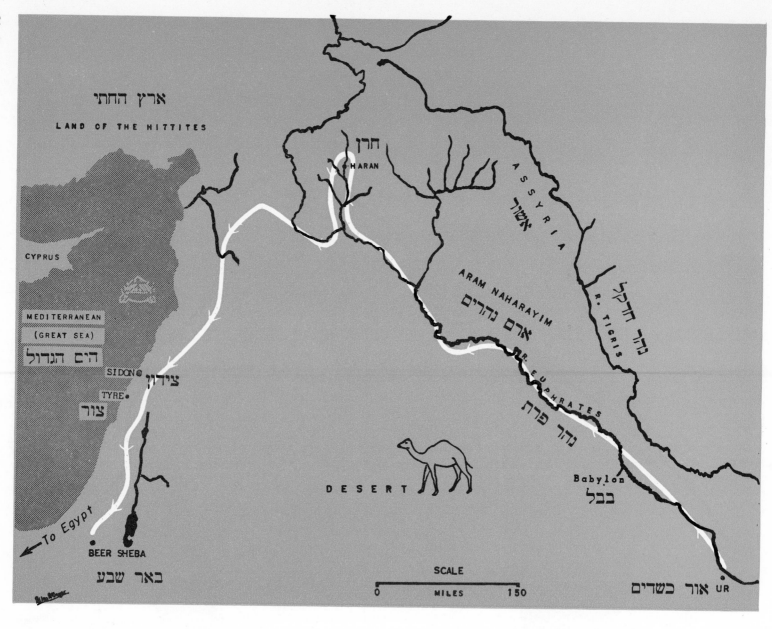

The Wanderings of the Patriarchs

Some few thousand years ago, the known world was a small one, centering on the "Fertile Crescent" of the Middle East. The two major civilisations of consequence in the area were those of Mesopotamia (the area between the two rivers, Tigris and Euphrates) and Egypt. Between the two, and on the main trade routes, lay a small country, the Land of Canaan, wherein lived a number of semi-nomadic tribes.

With the rise and fall of the various empires of the Middle East and, later, with the growth of the Greek and Roman Empires, the strategic importance of this part of the world increased greatly.

It was to this small area of the globe, seemingly insignificant and of little consequence, that Abraham travelled. There he settled and there the history of the Hebrew people commenced.

1 Abraham

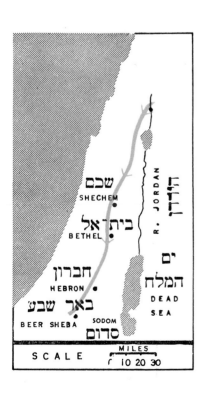

1   "And Terah took Abram his son, and Lot the son of Haran, his son's son, and Sarai his daughter-in-law, his son Abram's wife; and they went forth with them from Ur of the Chaldees, to go into the land of Canaan; and they came unto Haran, and dwelt there." Gen. 11 (31).

2   "And Abram took Sarai his wife, and Lot his brother's son, and all their substance that they had gathered, and the souls that they had gotten in Haran; and they went forth to go into the Land of Canaan, and into the Land of Canaan they came." Gen. 12 (5).

3   "And Abram passed through the land unto the place of Shechem. . . ." Gen. 12 (6).

4   "And he removed from thence unto the mountain on the east of Beth-el." Gen. 12 (8).

5   "And Abram journeyed, going on still toward the South." Gen. 12 (9).

6   "And there was a famine in the land and Abram went down into Egypt to sojourn there. . . ." Gen. 12 (10).

7   "And Abram went up out of Egypt, he, and his wife, and all that he had, and Lot with him into the South." Gen. 13 (1).

8   "And he went on his journeys from the South even to Beth-el, unto the place where his tent had been at the beginning. . . ." Gen. 13 (3).

9   "So Lot chose him all the plain of the Jordan; and Lot journeyed east." Gen. . . . 13 (11).

10   ". . . and Lot dwelt in the cities of the plain, and moved his tent as far as Sodom." Gen. 13 (12).

11   "And Abram moved his tent, and came and dwelt by the terebinths of Mamre which are in Hebron . . ." Gen. 13 (18).

12   "And Abraham journeyed thence toward the land of the South. . . ." Gen. 20 (1).

13   ". . . and Abraham dwelt at Beer-sheba." Gen. 22 (19).

14   "And Sarah died in Kiriath-arba—the same is Hebron. . . ." Gen. 23 (2).

15   ". . . For he (Isaac) dwelt in the land of the South." Gen. 24 (62).

16   "And he went up from thence to Beer-sheba." Gen. 26 (23).

2 Jacob

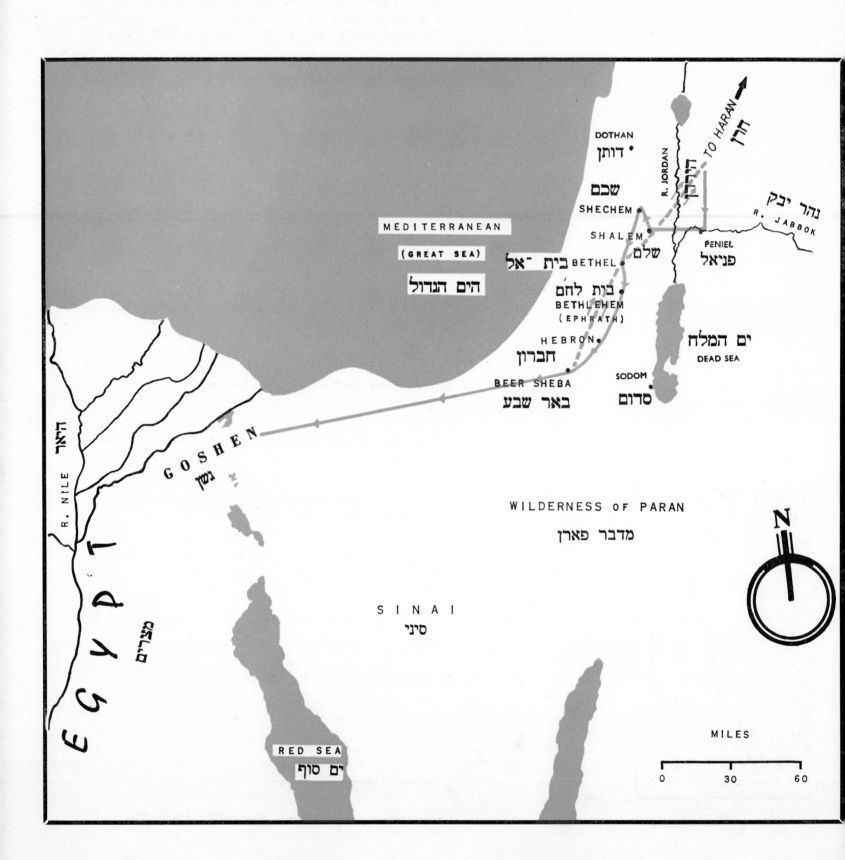

MEDITERRANEAN

(GREAT SEA)

הים הגדול

DOTHAN
דותן

שכם
SHECHEM

SHALEM
שלם

בית-אל BETHEL

בית לחם
BETHLEHEM
(EPHRATH)

HEBRON
חברון

BEER SHEBA
באר שבע

R. JORDAN

הירדן

TO HARAN

חרן

נהר יבק
R. JABBOK

PENIEL
פניאל

ים המלח
DEAD SEA

SODOM
סדום

GOSHEN גשן

EGYPT

R. NILE
היאור

WILDERNESS OF PARAN
מדבר פארן

N

SINAI
סיני

RED SEA
ים סוף

MILES

0   30   60

Jacob's Journey to Haran

"Now, therefore, my son, hearken to my voice, and arise, flee thou to Laban my brother to Haran." Gen. 27 (43).

"Arise, go to Paddan-aram. . . ." Gen. 28 (2).
Note: Paddan-aram is generally identified with the area of Haran.

"And Jacob went out from Beer-sheba and went toward Haran." Gen. 28 (10).

"And he lighted upon the place, and tarried there all night. . . ." Gen. 28 (11).

"And he called the name of that place Beth-el, but the name of the city was Luz at first." Gen. 28 (19).

Jacob's Return from Haran

". . . and he rose up, and passed over the River . . ." Gen. 31 (21).
Note: The river referred to is the Euphrates.

"And he rose up that night, and took his two wives, and his two handmaids, and his eleven children, and passed over the ford of the Jabbok." Gen. 32 (23). AV: 32 (22)

"And Jacob called the name of the place Peniel. . . ." Gen. 32 (31). AV: 32 (30)
Note: "Peniel" is sometimes referred to as "Penuel".

"And Jacob came to Shalem, a city of Shechem, which is in the land of Canaan. . . ." Gen. 33 (18).
Note: Some authorities translate "Shalem" as "in peace" and do not identify a city by this name.

"And God said unto Jacob: Arise, go up to Beth-el, and dwell there. . . ." Gen. 35 (1).

"So Jacob came to Luz, which is in the land of Canaan—the same is Beth-el. . . ." Gen. 35 (6).

"And they journeyed from Beth-el; and there was still some way to come to Ephrath. . . ." Gen. 35 (16).

"And Rachel died, and was buried in the way to Ephrath—the same is Bethlehem." Gen. 35 (19).

"And Jacob came unto Isaac his father to Mamre, to Kiriath-arba—the same is Hebron—where Abraham and Isaac sojourned." Gen. 35 (27).

Joseph's Travels

"And his (Joseph's) brethren went to feed their father's flock in Shechem." Gen. 37 (12).

". . . and he (Joseph) came to Shechem." Gen. 37 (14).

". . . and Joseph went after his brethren, and found them in Dothan." Gen. 37 (17).

". . . and they brought Joseph into Egypt." Gen. 37 (28).

Jacob's Journey into Egypt

"And Israel took his journey with all that he had, and came to Beer-sheba . . ." Gen. 46 (1).

"And Jacob rose up from Beer-sheba; and the sons of Israel carried Jacob their father, and their little ones, and their wives, in the wagons which Pharaoh had sent to carry them." Gen. 46 (5).

". . . and came into Egypt, Jacob, and all his seed with him." Gen. 46 (6).

". . . and they came into the land of Goshen." Gen. 46 (28).

"And Israel dwelt in the land of Egypt, in the land of Goshen; and they got them possessions therein, and were fruitful, and multiplied exceedingly." Gen. 47 (27).

The Exodus

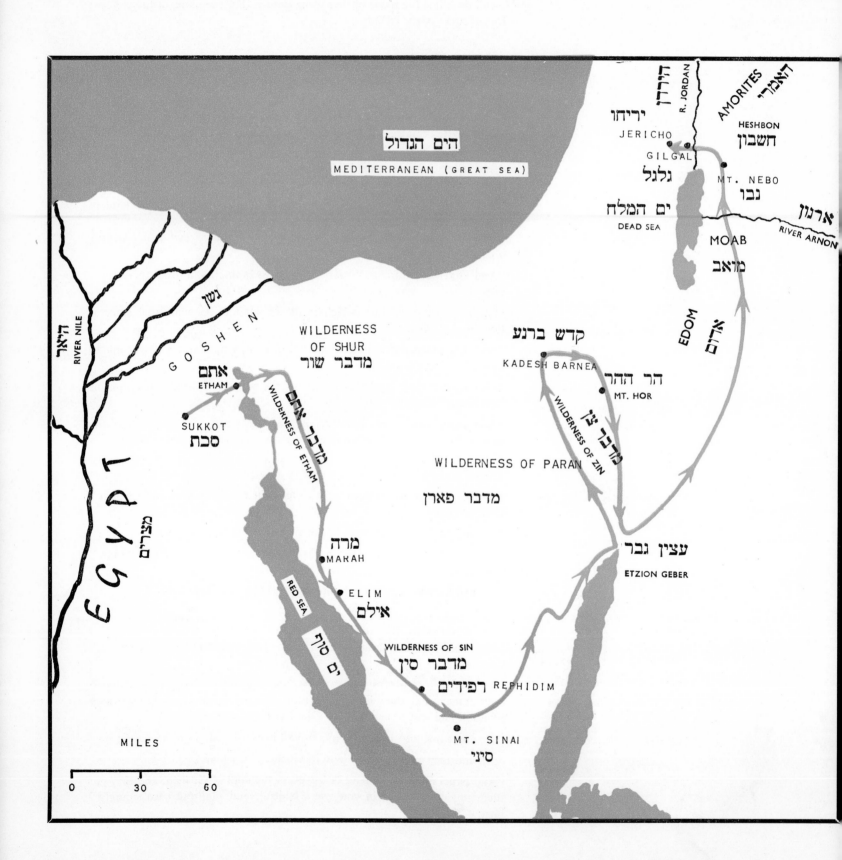

MEDITERRANEAN (GREAT SEA)

הים הגדול

ירדן R. JORDAN

AMORITES האמרי

יריחו JERICHO

HESHBON חשבון

גלגל GILGAL

MT. NEBO נבו

ים המלח DEAD SEA

ארנון ARNON

RIVER ARNON

MOAB מואב

EDOM אדום

RIVER NILE יאר

GOSHEN גשן

WILDERNESS OF SHUR מדבר שור

קדש ברנע KADESH BARNEA

אתם ETHAM

WILDERNESS OF ETHAM מדבר אתם

הר ההר MT. HOR

SUKKOT סכת

WILDERNESS OF ZIN מדבר צן

EGYPT מצרים

WILDERNESS OF PARAN מדבר פארן

מרה MARAH

עצין גבר ETZION GEBER

ELIM אילם

RED SEA ים סוף

WILDERNESS OF SIN מדבר סין

רפידים REPHIDIM

MT. SINAI סיני

MILES

0   30   60

"And they took their journey from Sukkot and encamped in Etham, on the edge of the wilderness." Exodus 13 (20).

Crossing of the Red Sea

"And they journeyed . . . and passed through the midst of the sea into the wilderness. . . ." Numbers 33 (8).

Three days without water

"And Moses led Israel onward from the Red Sea, and they went out into the Wilderness of Shur." Exodus 15 (22).

Episode of the Bitter Waters

". . . And they went three days' journey in the Wilderness of Etham, and pitched in Marah." Numbers 33 (8).

"And they journeyed from Marah, and came unto Elim. . . ." Numbers 33 (9).

"And they journeyed from Elim, and pitched by the Red Sea." Numbers 33 (10).

Commencement of the Manna

"And all the congregation of the children of Israel came unto the Wilderness of Sin, which is between Elim and Sinai, on the fifteenth day of the second month after their departing out of the land of Egypt." Exodus 16 (1).
Note: Certain intermediate places are mentioned (see Numbers 33 (13, 14)) which cannot be identified with any degree of accuracy.

War with the Amalekites

"And all the congregation of the children of Israel journeyed from the Wilderness of Sin . . . and encamped in Rephidim and there was no water for the people to drink." Exodus 17 (1).

Giving of the Ten Commandments.
Incident of the Golden Calf

"And when they were departed from Rephidim and were come to the Wilderness of Sinai, they encamped in the wilderness and there Israel encamped before the mount." Exodus 19 (2).

Incident of the Quails

"And they journeyed from the Wilderness of Sinai . . ." Numbers 33 (16).
Note: Certain intermediate places are mentioned (see Numbers 33 (16–34)) which cannot be identified with any degree of accuracy.

"And they journeyed from Abronah, and pitched in Etzion-geber." Numbers 33 (35).

Sending of the 12 Spies
Death of Miriam
Striking the Rock

"And they journeyed from Etzion-geber and pitched in the Wilderness of Zin—the same is Kadesh." Numbers 33 (36).
Note: Kadesh is also referred to as Kadesh Barnea (see Deut. 1 (19).)

Death of Aaron

"And they journeyed from Kadesh and pitched in Mount Hor, on the edge of the land of Edom." Numbers 33 (37).
Note: Certain intermediate places are mentioned (see Deut. 10 (6, 7), Numbers 21 and Numbers 33 (41–47)), which cannot be identified with any degree of accuracy.

"And they journeyed from Mount Hor by the way to the Red Sea, to compass the land of Edom . . ." Numbers 21 (4).

"From thence they journeyed, and pitched on the other side of the Arnon, which is in the wilderness, that cometh out of the border of the Amorites—for Arnon is the border of Moab, between Moab and the Amorites." Numbers 21 (13).

Incident of Balak and Balaam

"And the children of Israel journeyed, and pitched in the plains of Moab beyond the Jordan at Jericho." Numbers 22 (1).
Note: i.e. on the east of the River Jordan.

Death of Moses

"And Moses went up from the plains of Moab unto Mount Nebo, to the top of Pisgah, that is over against Jericho. And the Lord showed him all the land . . ." Deut. 34 (1).
Note: The Hebrew "Pisgah" can be interpreted as meaning the "peak", i.e. the highest point of Mount Nebo.

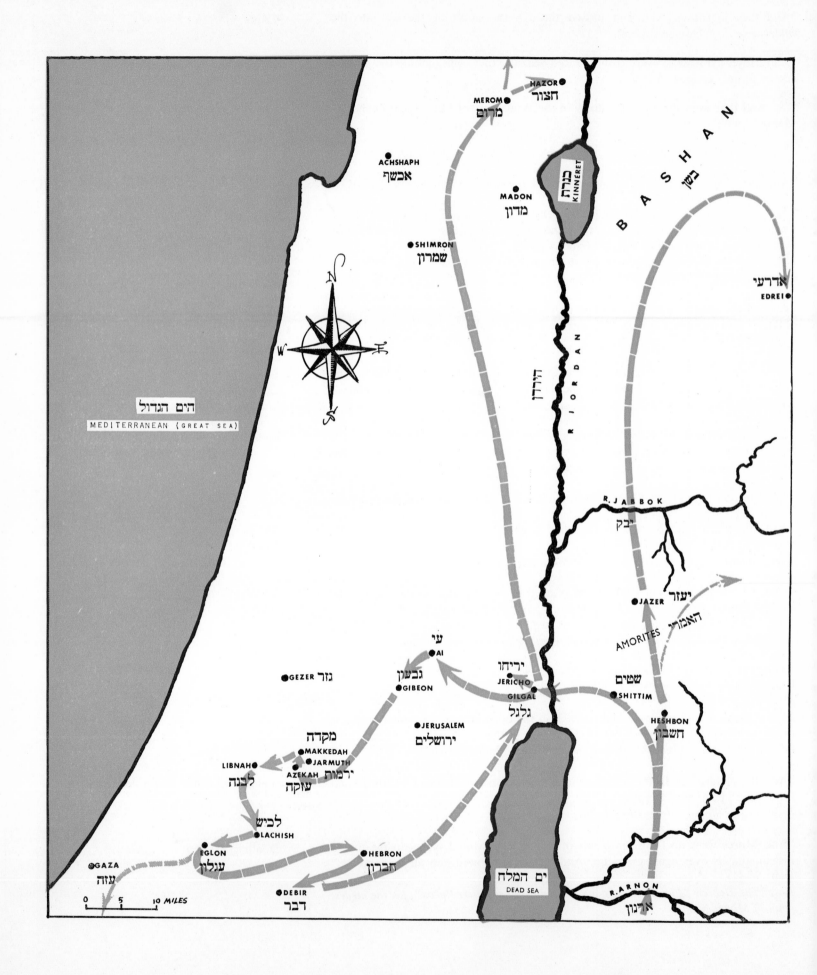

HAZOR חצור

MEROM מרום

ACHSHAPH אכשף

MADON מדון

BASHAN בשן

KINNERET כנרת

SHIMRON שמרון

EDREI אדרעי

N

W   E

S

R. IORDAN הירדן

הים הגדול

MEDITERRANEAN (GREAT SEA)

R. JABBOK יבק

JAZER יעזר

AMORITES האמרי

AI עי

GIBEON גבעון

GEZER גזר

JERICHO יריחו

SHITTIM שטים

JERUSALEM ירושלים

GILGAL גלגל

MAKKEDAH מקדה

JARMUTH ירמות

HESHBON חשבון

LIBNAH לבנה

AZEKAH עזקה

LACHISH לכיש

HEBRON חברון

EGLON עגלון

ים המלח
DEAD SEA

GAZA עזה

DEBIR דבר

R. ARNON ארנון

0 5 10 MILES

Conquest of the Land East of the Jordan

"And Israel smote him with the edge of the sword and possessed his land from the Arnon unto Jabbok even unto the children of Ammon . . ." Numbers 21 (24).
Note: Sihon, king of the Amorites, is referred to here.
"And Israel took all these cities; and Israel dwelt in all the cities of the Amorites, in Heshbon and in all the cities thereof." Numbers 21 (25).
"And Moses sent to spy out Jazer, and they took the towns thereof, and drove out the Amorites that were there." Numbers 21 (32).
"And they turned and went by the way of Bashan; and Og the king of Bashan went out against them, he and all his people to battle at Edrei." Numbers 21 (33).
"So they smote him . . . and possessed his land." Numbers 21 (35).
Note: See also Deuteronomy 3 (1–7).
Note: The tribes of Reuben and Gad and half the tribe of Manasseh occupied these areas of Trans-Jordan which had been captured. See Numbers 32. See also p. 21—"Division of the Land Among the Tribes".

River Arnon
to
River Jabbok
Land of Amorites
Heshbon
Jazer

Bashan
Edrei

Crossing of the Jordan

"And Joshua the son of Nun sent out of Shittim two spies secretly saying: 'Go view the land, and Jericho'. . . ." Joshua 2 (1).
"And Joshua rose early in the morning, and they removed from Shittim, and came to the Jordan . . ." Joshua 3 (1).
"And the priests that bore the ark of the covenant of the Lord stood firm on dry ground in the midst of the Jordan, while all Israel passed over on dry ground, until all the nation were passed clean over Jordan." Joshua 3 (17).
"And the people came up out of the Jordan on the tenth day of the first month, and encamped in Gilgal, on the east border of Jericho." Joshua 4 (19).
Note: Gilgal served Joshua as a base camp for the whole campaign in Southern Canaan.

Shittim

River Jordan

Gilgal

Conquest of Southern Canaan

". . . the people went up into the city, every man straight before him, and they took the city." Joshua 6 (20).
Note: The full account of the fall of Jericho is to be found in Joshua 6.
"And Joshua sent men from Jericho to Ai . . . saying, 'Go up and spy out the land'. . . ." Joshua 7 (2).
Note: The full account of the capture of Ai is to be found in Joshua 8 (1–29).
"And the children of Israel journeyed, and came unto their cities . . ." Joshua 9 (17).
Note: The full account of the Gibeonites is to be found in Joshua 9.
At Gibeon there took place a battle between the Israelites and the kings of Jerusalem, Hebron, Jarmuth, Lachish and Eglon. See Joshua 10.
". . . And they chased them . . . and smote them to Azekah and unto Makkedah." Joshua 10 (10).
"And Joshua passed from Makkedah, and all Israel with him, unto Libnah, and fought against Libnah." Joshua 10 (29).
"And Joshua passed from Libnah, and all Israel with him, unto Lachish . . ." Joshua 10 (31).
Note: The king of Gezer also fought against Joshua at Lachish. See Joshua 10 (33).
"And Joshua passed from Lachish, and all Israel with him, unto Eglon . . ." Joshua 10 (34).
"And Joshua went up from Eglon, and all Israel with him, unto Hebron . . ." Joshua 10 (36).
"And Joshua turned back, and all Israel with him, to Debir . . ." Joshua 10 (38).
"So Joshua smote all the land, the hill country, and the south, and the lowland and the slopes . . . and Joshua smote them from Kadesh-barnea even unto Gaza . . ." Joshua 10 (40, 41).
Note: For the location of Kadesh-barnea, see p. 16—"The Exodus".
"And Joshua returned, and all Israel with him, unto the camp to Gilgal." Joshua 10 (43).

Jericho

Ai

Gibeon

Azekah
Makkedah
Libnah
Lachish

Eglon
Hebron
Debir

Conquest of Northern Canaan

"And all the kings met together; and they came and pitched together at the waters of Merom, to fight with Israel." Joshua 11 (5).
Note: i.e. the kings of Hazor, Madon, Shimron, Achshaph, kings of the north, the Aravah south of Kinneret etc., etc. See Joshua 11 (1–3).
Note: Some authorities identify the waters of Merom with Lake Hulah.
"And the Lord delivered them into the hand of Israel, and they smote them, and chased them . . ." Joshua 11 (8).
"And Joshua turned back at that time and took Hazor . . . for Hazor beforetime was the head of all those kingdoms." Joshua 11 (10).
"So Joshua took all that land, the hill country . . . even unto Baal-gad in the valley of Lebanon under Mount Hermon . . ." Joshua 11 (16–17).
"So Joshua took the whole land . . . and the land had rest from war." Joshua 11 (23).
Note: Certain territory still remained to be captured. See Joshua 13 (1–6) and Judges 1.

Merom

Hazor

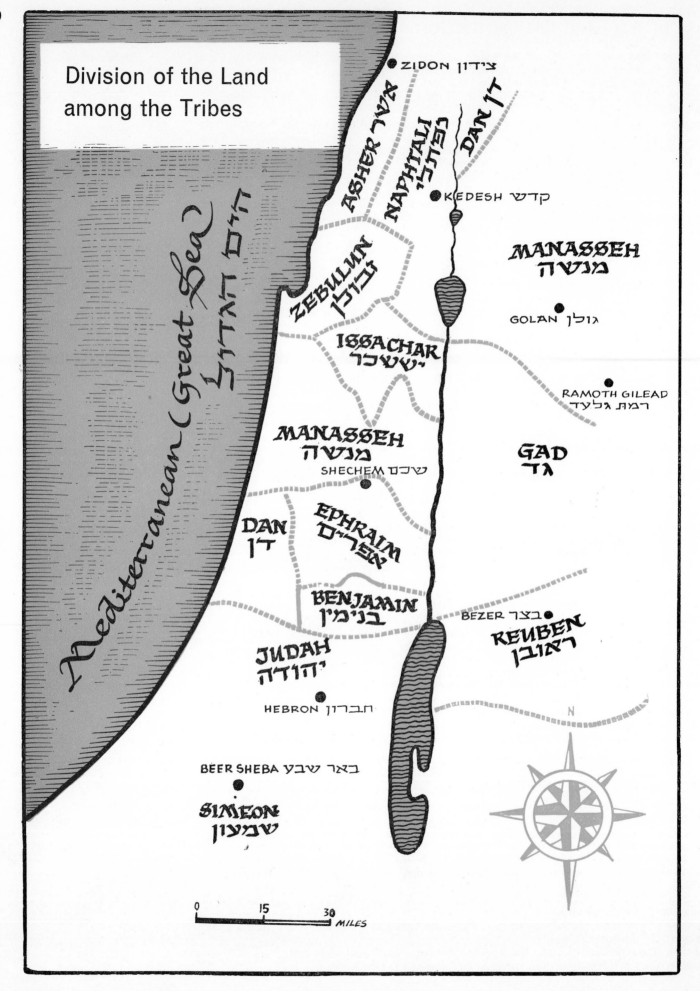

Division of the Land
among the Tribes

Mediterranean (Great Sea) הים הגדול

ZIDON צידון

ASHER אשר

NAPHTALI נפתלי

DAN דן

KEDESH קדש

MANASSEH מנשה

ZEBULUN זבולן

GOLAN גולן

ISSACHAR יששכר

RAMOTH GILEAD רמת גלעד

MANASSEH מנשה

SHECHEM שכם

GAD גד

DAN דן

EPHRAIM אפרים

BENJAMIN בנימין

BEZER בצר

REUBEN ראובן

JUDAH יהודה

HEBRON חברון

BEER SHEBA באר שבע

SIMEON שמעון

N

0   15   30
MILES

East of the Jordan

"And we took the land . . . beyond the Jordan, from the valley of Arnon unto Mount Hermon . . . all the cities of the plain, and all Gilead, and all Bashan . . . and this land . . . from Aroer, which is by the valley of Arnon, and half the hill country of Gilead, and the cities thereof, gave I unto the Reubenites and to the Gadites; and the rest of Gilead, and all Bashan, the kingdom of Og, gave I unto the half-tribe of Manasseh." Deut. 3 (8–13). *See also Numbers 32 (33).*
TRIBE OF REUBEN. See Joshua 13 (15–23).
TRIBE OF GAD. See Joshua 13 (24–28).
HALF-TRIBE OF MANASSEH. See Joshua 13 (29–31).

West of the Jordan

"Now therefore divide this land for an inheritance unto the nine tribes, and the half-tribe of Manasseh." Joshua 13 (7).
TRIBE OF JUDAH. See Joshua 15.
TRIBE OF EPHRAIM. See Joshua 16 (5–10). It will be noted that the Tribe of Ephraim had certain cities which actually lay within the territory of Manasseh.
HALF-TRIBE OF MANASSEH. See Joshua 17. It will be noted that Manasseh had certain cities which actually lay within the territory of Issachar and Asher.
TRIBE OF BENJAMIN. See Joshua 18 (11–28).
TRIBE OF SIMEON. See Joshua 19 (1–9). It will be noted (Joshua 19 (9)) that the portion of Simeon actually lay within the territory of Judah.
TRIBE OF ZEBULUN. See Joshua 19 (10–16).
TRIBE OF ISSACHAR. See Joshua 19 (17–23).
TRIBE OF ASHER. See Joshua 19 (24–31).
TRIBE OF NAPHTALI. See Joshua 19 (32–39).
TRIBE OF DAN. See Joshua 19 (40–48). The original portion allocated to the Tribe of Dan proved too small for them. Subsequently, the tribe moved northwards and captured the territory round Leshem (or Laish). (See Joshua 19 (47).) This is situated right in the north of Israel, at the source of the Jordan. It was referred to in Biblical times as being the northernmost point of the country, hence the phrase "from Dan to Beer-sheba". (See I Kings 5 (5). AV: 4 (25).

The Priests and Levites

"And the Lord said unto Aaron: 'Thou shalt have no inheritance in their land, neither shalt thou have any portion among them; for I am thy portion and thine inheritance among the children of Israel'." Numbers 18 (20).
"Only unto the tribe of Levi he gave no inheritance. . . ." Joshua 13 (14).
Note: Although the Priests and Levites were given no tribal territory, a number of cities within the territory of the other tribes was allocated to them.
"Command the children of Israel that they give unto the Levites of the inheritance of their possession cities to dwell in . . ." Numbers 35 (2).
"All the cities which ye shall give to the Levites shall be forty and eight cities . . ." Numbers 35 (7).
Note: Six of these forty-eight cities were "Cities of Refuge". See below. The towns are all listed in Joshua 21.

Cities of refuge

"When ye pass over the Jordan into the land of Canaan, then shall ye appoint you cities to be cities of refuge . . . there shall be for you six cities . . . three cities beyond the Jordan, and three cities shall ye give in the land of Canaan . . ." Numbers 35 (10–14).
Note: The purpose of the cities of refuge was to act as an asylum for a person who accidentally committed homicide. See Numbers 35 (15 onwards) and Joshua 20 (1–6).

The following towns were appointed. (*See Joshua 20 (7–9).*)

West of the Jordan: KEDESH in the territory of Naphtali
SHECHEM in the territory of Ephraim
HEBRON in the territory of Judah

East of the Jordan BEZER in the territory of Reuben
RAMOTH-GILEAD in the territory of Gad
GOLAN in the territory of Manasseh

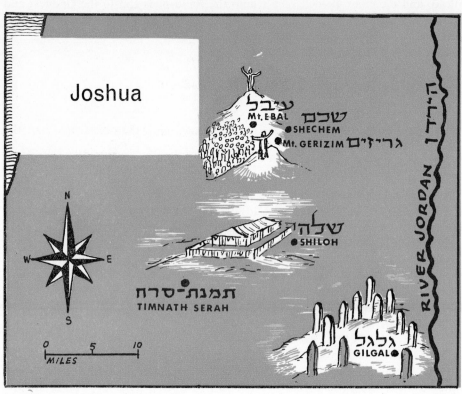

Note: The home of Shamgar is assumed to be at Beth-Anath

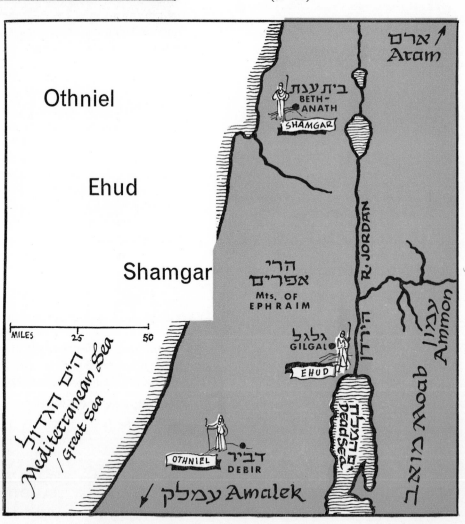

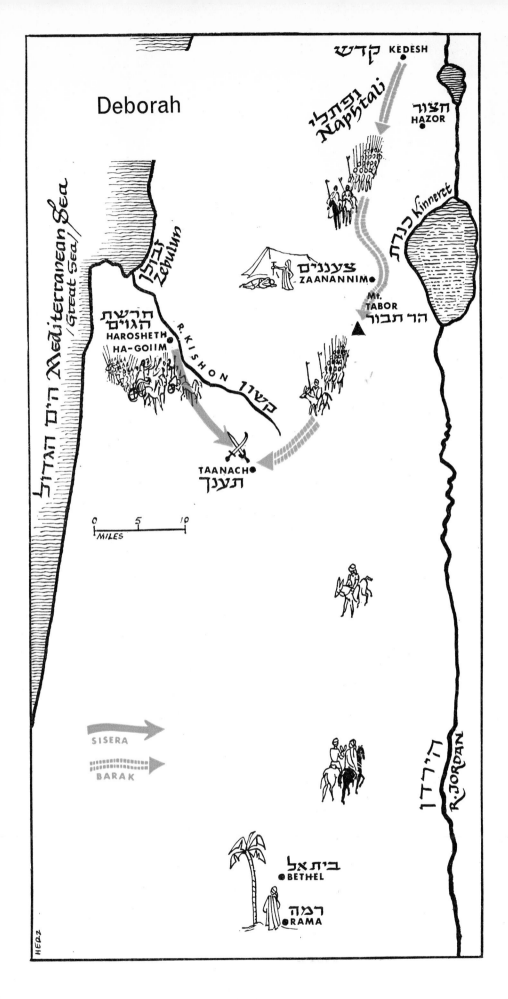

Deborah

"And the children of Israel again did that which was evil in the sight of the Lord, when Ehud was dead. And the Lord gave them over into the hand of Jabin, King of Canaan, that reigned in Hazor; the captain of whose host was Sisera, who dwelt in Harosheth-hagoiim." Judges 4 (1–2).

"And she (Deborah) sat under the palm-tree of Deborah between Ramah and Beth-el in mount Ephraim." Judges 4 (5).

"And she sent and called Barak the son of Abinoam out of Kedesh-naphtali, and said unto him . . . 'Go and draw toward Mount Tabor'. . . ." Judges 4 (6). "And Deborah arose, and went with Barak to Kedesh." Judges 4 (9).

"And Sisera gathered together all his chariots . . . From Harosheth-hagoiim unto the brook of Kishon." Judges 4 (13). *Note:— According to The Song of Deborah (Judges 5 v. 19) the actual location of the battle was at Taanach.*

"So Barak went down from Mount Tabor . . ." Judges 4 (14). "And the Lord discomfited Sisera . . . and Sisera alighted from his chariot, and fled away on his feet." Judges 4 (15).

"But Barak pursued after the chariots, and after the host, unto Harosheth-hagoiim . . ." Judges 4 (16).

"Howbeit Sisera fled away on his feet to the tent of Jael the wife of Heber the Kenite . . ." Judges 4 (17). *Note: According to Judges 4 (11) Heber the Kenite lived at Zaanannim.*

"Then Jael, Heber's wife, took a tent-pin . . . and smote the pin into his temples . . . so he swooned and died. And behold, as Barak pursued Sisera, Jael came out to meet him, and said unto him 'Come, and I will show thee the man whom thou seekest'. And he came unto her; and behold, Sisera lay dead, and the tent-pin was in his temples." Judges 4 (21–22).
For the "Song of Deborah" see Judges Chapter V.

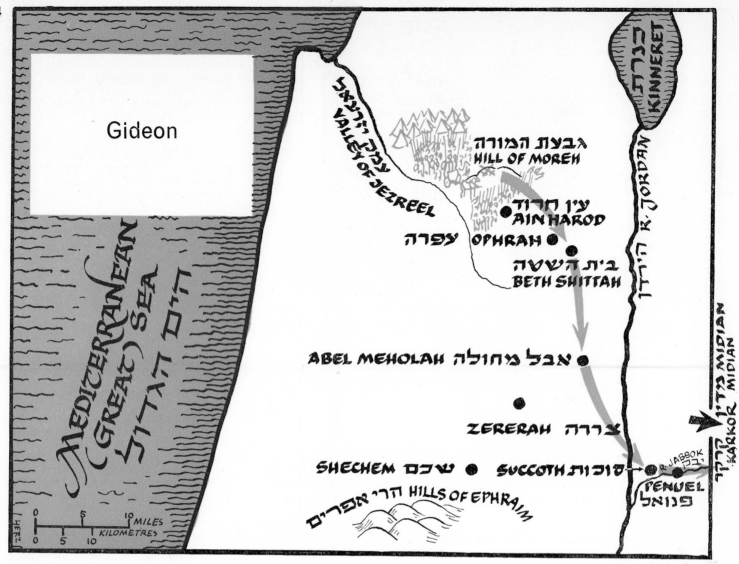

Gideon

כנרת KINNERET

עמק יזראל VALLEY OF JEZREEL

גבעת המורה HILL OF MOREH

עין חרוד AIN HAROD

עפרה OPHRAH

ב'ת השטה BETH SHITTAH

ר' הירדן R. JORDAN

אבל מחולה ABEL MEHOLAH

צררה ZERERAH

שכם SHECHEM · סוכות SUCCOTH

יבק JABBOK

פנואל PENUEL

הרי אפרים HILLS OF EPHRAIM

מדבר מדין MIDIAN · קרקור מדין KARKOR MIDIAN

ים התיכון (הים הגדול) MEDITERRANEAN (GREAT) SEA

MILES
KILOMETRES
0 5 10

HERZ

For the early life of Gideon—See Judges 6 (11–32).

"Now all the Midianites and the Amalekites and the children of the east assembled themselves together; and they passed over, and pitched in the valley of Jezreel." Judges 6 (33).

"Then Jerubbaal, who is Gideon, and all the people that were with him, rose up early, and pitched beside Ain-harod; and the camp of Midian was on the north side of them, by the Hill of Moreh, in the valley." Judges 7 (1).
The story of how Gideon selected his army by the drinking test is told in Judges 7 (2–8).
The account of the course of the battle is told in Judges 7 (9–21).

". . . and the host fled as far as Beth-shittah toward Zererah, as far as the border of Abel-meholah, by Tabbath." Judges 7 (22).

"And the men of Israel were gathered together out of Naphtali, and out of Asher, and out of all Manasseh, and pursued after Midian." Judges 7 (23).

"And Gideon sent messengers throughout all the hill country of Ephraim, saying: 'Come down against Midian, and take before them the waters, as far as Beth-barah, and also the Jordan.'" Judges 7 (24).

"And Gideon came to the Jordan, and passed over, he, and the three hundred men that were with him, faint, yet pursuing." Judges 8 (4).

"And he said unto the men of Succoth: 'Give, I pray you, loaves of bread unto the people that follow me; for they are faint, and I am pursuing after Zebah and Zalmunna, the kings of Midian'." Judges 8 (5).

"And he went up thence to Penuel . . ." Judges 8 (8).

"Now Zebah and Zalmunna were in Karkor . . . And Gideon went up . . . and smote the host; for the host was secure." Judges 8 (10–11).

Gideon returned by way of Succoth and Penuel, and subsequently dwelt in his home town of Ophrah.

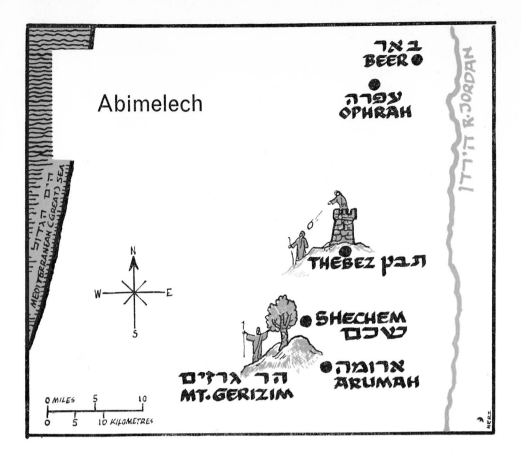

Abimelech

בְּאֵר BEER

עָפְרָה OPHRAH

R. JORDAN הַיַרְדֵּן

THEBEZ תֵּבֵץ

SHECHEM שְׁכֶם

אֲרוּמָה ARUMAH

הַר גְּרִזִים MT. GERIZIM

הַיָּם הַגָּדוֹל MEDITERRANEAN (GREAT) SEA

0 MILES 5 10
0 5 10 KILOMETRES

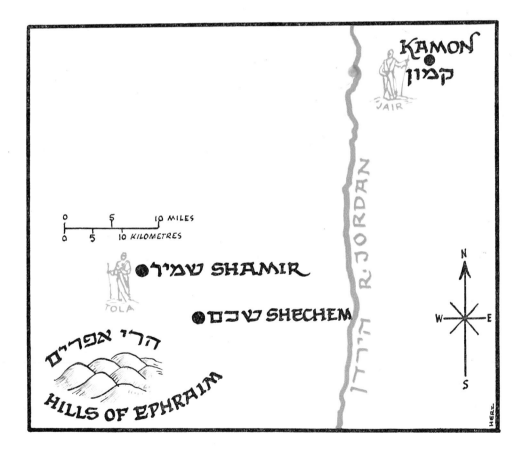

KAMON קָמוֹן

JAIR

R. JORDAN הַיַרְדֵּן

שָׁמִיר SHAMIR

TOLA

שְׁכֶם SHECHEM

הָרֵי אֶפְרַיִם HILLS OF EPHRAIM

0 5 10 MILES
0 5 10 KILOMETRES

Tola — See Judges 10 (1–2)

Jair — See Judges 10 (3–5)

"And Abimelech the son of Jerubbaal went to Shechem unto his mother's brethren . . ." Judges 9 (1).

"And he went unto his father's house at Ophrah, and slew his brethren the sons of Jerubbaal, being threescore and ten persons, upon one stone; but Jotham the youngest son of Jerubbaal was left; for he hid himself." Judges 9 (5).

"And all the men of Shechem assembled themselves together . . . and went and made Abimelech king, . . . in Shechem." Judges 9 (6).

"And when they told it to Jotham, he went and stood at the top of Mount Gerizim, and lifted up his voice, and cried, and said unto them: 'Hearken unto me, ye men of Shechem, that God may hearken unto you'." Judges 9 (7). (*Note: The parable of the trees is found in Judges 9 (8–20).*)

"And Jotham ran away, and fled, and went to Beer, and dwelt there, for fear of Abimelech his brother." Judges 9 (21).

"And Abimelech rose up, and all the people that were with him, by night, and they lay in wait against Shechem in four companies." Judges 9 (34).

"And Gaal went out before the men of Shechem, and fought with Abimelech." Judges 9 (39). "And Abimelech chased him, and he fled before him, and there fell many wounded, even unto the entrance of the gate." Judges 9 (40).

"And Abimelech dwelt at Arumah . . ." Judges 9 (41).
The struggle against the people of Shechem, culminating in the fire of the Tower of Shechem, is told in Judges 9 (42–49).

"Then went Abimelech to Thebez, and encamped against Thebez, and took it. But there was a strong tower within the city, and thither fled all the men and women, even all they of the city, and shut themselves in, and got them up to the roof of the tower." Judges 9 (50–51).

"And Abimelech came unto the tower, and fought against it, and went close unto the door of the tower to burn it with fire. And a certain woman cast a piece of millstone upon Abimelech's head and broke his skull." Judges 9 (52, 53).

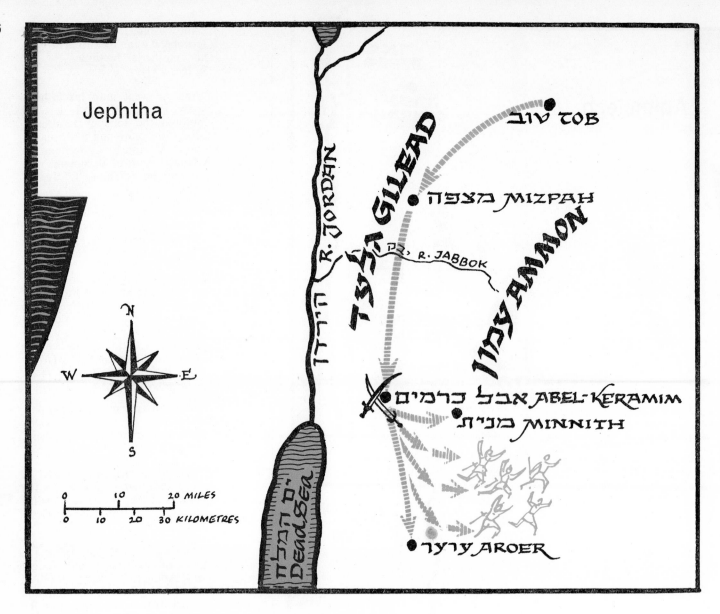

Jephtha

"Then Jephtha fled from his brethren, and dwelt in the land of Tob; and there were gathered vain fellows to Jephtha, and they went out with him. And it came to pass after a while, that the children of Ammon made war against Israel." Ju. 11 (3–4).

"Then Jephtha went with the elders of Gilead, and the people made him head and chief over them; and Jephtha spoke all his words before the Lord in Mizpah." Ju. 11 (11).

"And Jephtha vowed a vow unto the Lord, and said: 'If Thou wilt indeed deliver the children of Ammon into my hand, then it shall be, that whatsoever cometh forth of the doors of my house to meet me, when I return in peace from the children of Ammon, it shall be the Lord's, and I will offer it up for a burnt-offering'." Ju. 11 (30–31).

"So Jephtha passed over unto the children of Ammon to fight against them; and the Lord delivered them into his hand." Ju. 11 (32).

"And he smote them from Aroer until thou come to Minnith, even twenty cities, and unto Abel-Keramim, with a very great slaughter. So the children of Ammon were subdued before the children of Israel." Ju. 11 (33).

"And Jephtha came to Mizpah unto his house, and behold, his daughter came out to meet him with timbrels and with dances; and she was his only child; beside her he had neither son nor daughter." Ju. 11 (34).

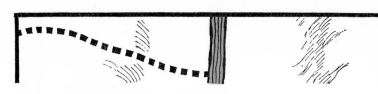

The War against the Ephraimites

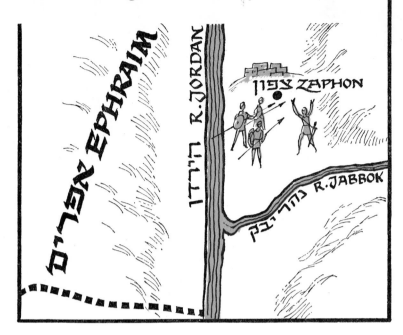

"And the men of Ephraim were gathered together, and passed to Zaphon; and they said unto Jephtha: 'Wherefore didst thou pass over to fight against the children of Ammon, and didst not call us to go with thee? We will burn thy house upon thee with fire'." Ju. 12 (1).

"Then Jephtha gathered together all the men of Gilead, and fought with Ephraim; and the men of Gilead smote Ephraim, because they said: 'Ye are fugitives of Ephraim, ye Gileadites, in the midst of Ephraim, and in the midst of Manasseh'." Ju. 12 (4).

"And the Gileadites took the fords of the Jordan against the Ephraimites; and it was so, that when any of the fugitives of Ephraim said: 'Let me go over', the men of Gilead said unto him: 'Art thou an Ephraimite?' If he said: 'Nay'; then said they unto him: 'Say now Shibboleth'; and he said 'Sibboleth'; for he could not frame to pronounce it right; and they laid hold on him, and slew him at the fords of the Jordan; and there fell at that time of Ephraim forty and two thousand." Ju. 12 (5–6).

Ibzan   See Judges 12 (8–10)

Elon   See Judges 12 (11–12)

Abdon   See Judges 12 (13–15)

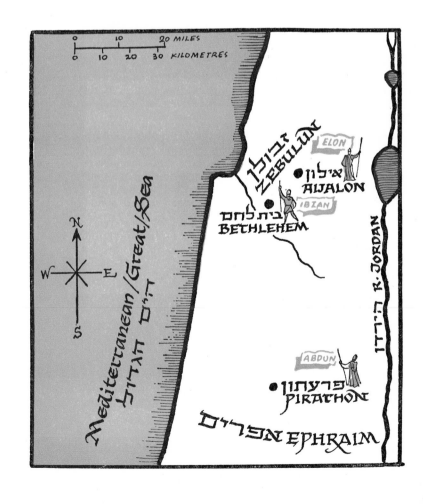

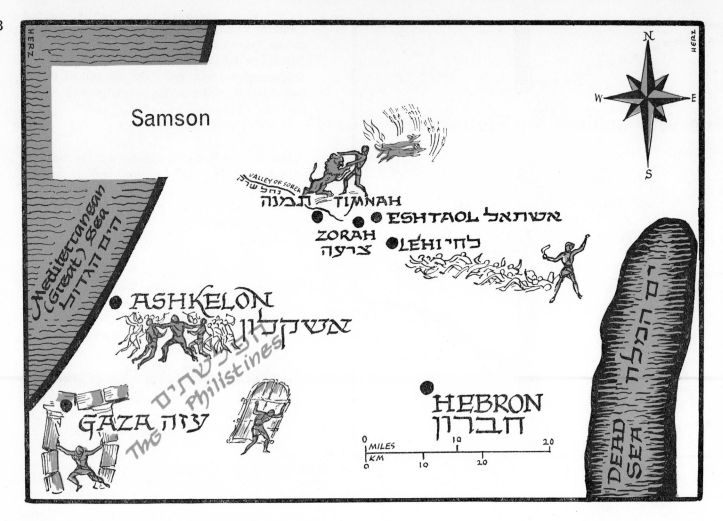

"And the children of Israel again did that which was evil in the sight of the Lord; and the Lord delivered them into the hand of the Philistines forty years." Ju. 13 (1).

"And the woman bore a son, and called his name Samson; and the child grew, and the Lord blessed him. And the spirit of the Lord began to move him in Mahaneh-dan, between Zorah and Eshtaol." Ju. 13 (24–25).

"Then went Samson down, and his father and his mother, to Timnah, and, came to the vineyards of Timnah; and, behold, a young lion roare against him. And the spirit of the Lord came mightily upon him, and he rent him as one would have rent a kid, and he had nothing in hand; but he told not his father or his mother what he had done." Ju. 14 (5–6).

"And the spirit of the Lord came mightily upon him, and he went down to Ashkelon, and smote thirty men of them . . ." Ju. 14 (19).

"And Samson went and caught three hundred foxes, and took torches, and turned tail to tail, and put a torch in the midst between every two tails." Ju. 15 (4).

"Then the Philistines went up, and pitched in Judah, spread themselves against Lehi." Ju. 15 (9).

"When he came unto Lehi, the Philistines shouted as they met him; and the spirit of the Lord came mightily upon him . . . And he found a new jawbone of an ass, and put forth his hand, and took it, and smote a thousand men therewith." Ju. 15 (14–15).

"And Samson went to Gaza . . . And Samson lay till midnight, and arose at midnight, and laid hold of the doors of the gate of the city, and the two posts, and plucked them up, bar and all, and put them upon his shoulders, and carried them up to the top of the mountain that is before Hebron." Ju. 16 (1 and 3).

"And it came to pass afterward, that he loved a woman in the valley of Sorek, whose name was Delilah." Ju. 16 (4). "And the Philistines laid hold on him, and put out his eyes; and they brought him down to Gaza, and bound him with fetters of brass; and he did grind in the prison-house." Ju. 16 (21).

"And the lords of the Philistines gathered them together to offer a great sacrifice unto Dagon their god . . . And they called for Samson out of the prison-house; and he made sport before them; and they set him between the pillars." Ju. 16 (23 and 25).

"And Samson took fast hold of the two middle pillars upon which the house rested, and leaned upon them, the one with his right hand, and the other with his left. And Samson said: 'Let me die with the Philistines'. And he bent with all his might; and the house fell upon the lords, and upon all the people that were therein. So the dead that he slew at his death were more than they that he slew in his life." Ju. 16 (29–30).

"Then his brethren and all the house of his father came down, and took him, and brought him up, and buried him between Zorah and Eshtaol in the burying-place of Manoah his father. And he judged Israel twenty years." Ju. 16 (31).

The Migration of the Tribe of Dan

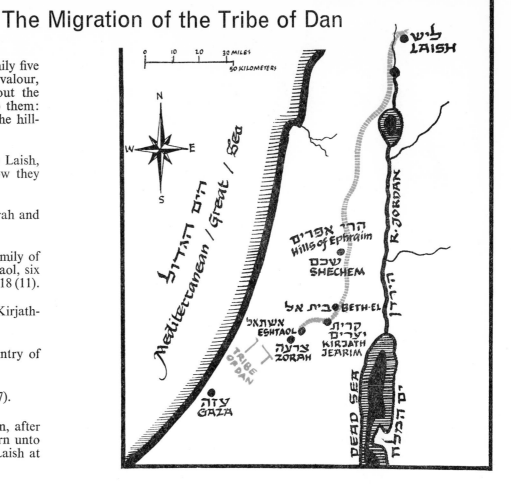

"And the children of Dan sent of their family five men from their whole number, men of valour, from Zorah, and from Eshtaol, to spy out the land, and to search it; and they said unto them: 'Go, search the land'; and they came to the hill-country of Ephraim . . ." Ju. 18 (2).

"Then the five men departed, and came to Laish, and saw the people that were therein, how they dwelt in security . . ." Ju. 18 (7).

"And they came unto their brethren to Zorah and Eshtaol . . ." Ju. 18 (8).

"And there set forth from thence of the family of the Danites, out of Zorah and out of Eshtaol, six hundred men girt with weapons of war." Ju. 18 (11).

"And they went up, and encamped in Kirjath-jearim, in Judah . . ." Ju. 18 (12).

"And they passed thence into the hill-country of Ephraim . . ." Ju. 18 (13).

"And they . . . came unto Laish." Ju. 18 (27).

"And they called the name of the city Dan, after the name of Dan their father, who was born unto Israel; howbeit the name of the city was Laish at the first." Ju. 18 (29).

The Battle with the Benjamites

"Then all the children of Israel went out, and the congregation was assembled as one man, from Dan even to Beer-sheba, with the land of Gilead, unto the Lord at Mizpah." Ju. 20 (1). *Note: Mizpah here is not identical with the Mizpah of Jephtha. See page 26*

"And the children of Benjamin gathered themselves together out of their cities unto Gibeah, to go out to battle against the children of Israel." Ju. 20 (14). "And the children of Israel arose, and went up to Beth-el, and asked counsel of God; and they said: 'Who shall go up for us first to battle against the children of Benjamin?' And the Lord said, 'Judah first'." Ju. 20 (18).

"And the men of Israel went out to battle against Benjamin; and the men of Israel set the battle in array against them at Gibeah." Ju. 20 (20).

"And there fell of Benjamin eighteen thousand men; all these were men of valour. And they turned and fled toward the wilderness unto the rock of Rimmon; and they gleaned of them in the highways five thousand men; and followed hard after them unto Gidom, and smote of them two thousand men." Ju. 20 (44–45).

Note: For the reconciliation with the Tribe of Benjamin, see Judges 21 (16–25).

Early Life

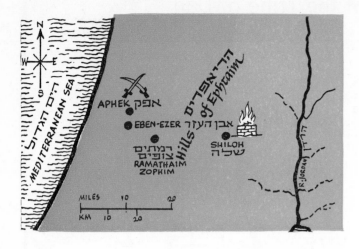

"Now there was a certain man of Ramathaim-zophim of the hill-country of Ephraim, and his name was Elkanah . . . And this man went up out of his city from year to year to worship and to sacrifice unto the Lord of hosts in Shiloh." I Sam. 1 (1, 3).

"And it came to pass . . . that Hannah conceived and bore a son and she called his name Samuel." I Sam. 1 (20).

"And when she had weaned him, she took him up with her . . . and brought him unto the house of the Lord in Shiloh; and the child was very young." I Sam. 1 (24).

"Now Israel went out against the Philistines to battle, and pitched beside Eben-ezer; and the Philistines pitched in Aphek." I Sam. 4 (1).

"And the Philistines fought, and Israel was smitten . . . And the ark of God was taken; and the two sons of Eli, Hophni and Phinehas, were slain." I Sam. 4 (10, 11).

Wandering of the Ark

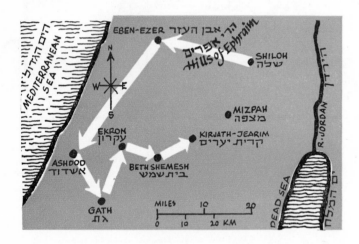

"Now the Philistines had taken the ark of God, and they brought it from Eben-ezer unto Ashdod." I Sam. 5 (1).

"They sent therefore and gathered all the lords of the Philistines unto them . . . And they answered: 'Let the ark of the God of Israel be carried about unto Gath.'" I Sam. 5 (8).

"So they sent the ark of God to Ekron. . . ." I Sam. 5 (10).

"And the kine took the straight way by the way to Beth-shemesh . . ." I Sam. 6 (12).

"And the men of Kirjath-jearim came, and fetched up the ark of the Lord, and brought it into the house of Abinadab in the hill, and sanctified Eleazar his son to keep the ark of the Lord." I Sam. 7 (1). *Note: The Ark remained here until it was removed to Jerusalem by David. See II Sam. 6 (12).*

Circuit of Samuel

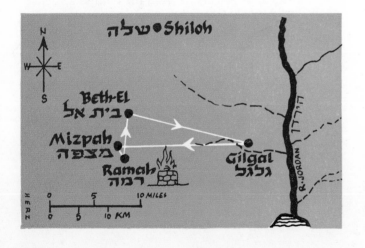

"And he went from year to year in circuit to Beth-el and Gilgal, and Mizpah; and he judged Israel in all those places." I Sam. 7 (16).

"And his return was to Ramah, for there was his house; and there he judged Israel; and he built there an altar unto the Lord." I Sam. 7 (17).

"Then all the elders of Israel gathered themselves together, and came to Samuel unto Ramah. And they said '. . . now make us a king to judge us like all the nations'." I Sam. 8 (4, 5).

"And the Lord said to Samuel: 'Hearken unto their voice, and make them a king'. . . ." I Sam. 8 (22).

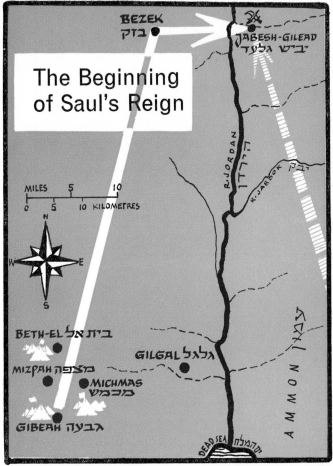

The Beginning of Saul's Reign

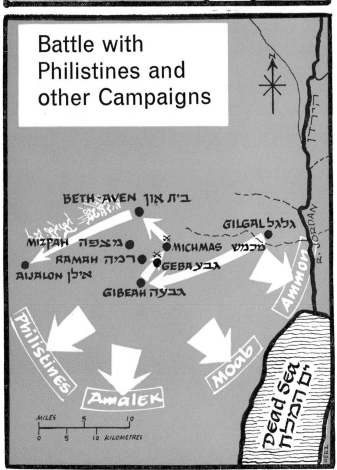

Battle with Philistines and other Campaigns

"And Samuel called the people together unto the Lord to Mizpah . . ." I Sam. 10 (17).

"And Samuel said to all the people: 'See ye him whom the Lord hath chosen, that there is none like him among all the people?' And all the people shouted, and said: 'Long live the king'." I Sam. 10 (24).

"And Saul also went to his house to Gibeah; and there went with him the men of valour, whose hearts God had touched." I Sam. 10 (26).

"Then Nahash the Ammonite came up, and encamped against Jabesh-gilead; and all the men of Jabesh said unto Nahash: 'Make a covenant with us, and we will serve thee'." I Sam. 11 (1).

"And he (Saul) numbered them in Bezek . . ." I Sam. 11 (8). "And it was so on the morrow . . . and they came into the midst of the camp in the morning watch, and smote the Ammonites . . ." I Sam. 11 (11).

"And all the people went to Gilgal; and there they made Saul king before the Lord in Gilgal; and there they sacrificed sacrifices of peace-offerings before the Lord; and there Saul and all the people of Israel rejoiced greatly." I Sam. 11 (15).

"And Saul chose him three thousand men of Israel; whereof two thousand were with Saul in Michmas and in the mount of Beth-el, and a thousand were with Jonathan in Gibeath-benjamin, and the rest of the people he sent every man to his tent." I Sam. 13 (2).

"And Jonathan smote the garrison of the Philistines that was in Geba, and the Philistines heard of it. . . ." I Sam. 13 (3).

"And all Israel heard say that Saul had smitten the garrison of the Philistines . . . And the people were gathered together after Saul to Gilgal." I Sam. 13(4) .

"And the Philistines assembled themselves together to fight with Israel, thirty thousand chariots, and six thousand horsemen, and people as the sand which is on the sea-shore in multitude; and they came up, and pitched in Michmas, eastward of Beth-aven." I Sam. 13 (5).

"And Saul, and Jonathan his son, and the people that were present with them, abode in Gibeath-benjamin, but the Philistines encamped in Michmas." I Sam. 13 (16).

"And Saul and all the people that were with him were gathered together, and came to the battle; and, behold, every man's sword was against his fellow, and there was a very great discomfiture." I Sam. 14 (20).

"So the Lord saved Israel that day; and the battle passed on as far as Beth-aven." I Sam. 14 (23).

"And they smote of the Philistines that day from Michmas to Aijalon . . ." I Sam. 14 (31).

"So Saul took the kingdom over Israel, and fought against all his enemies on every side, against Moab, and against the children of Ammon, and against Edom, and against the kings of Zobah, and against the Philistines; and whithersoever he turned himself, he put them to the worse. And he did valiantly, and smote the Amalekites, and delivered Israel out of the hands of them that spoiled them." I Sam. 14 (47, 48).

Note: For the description of Saul's battle with the Amalekites and the subsequent slaying of Agag by Samuel, see I Sam. 15.

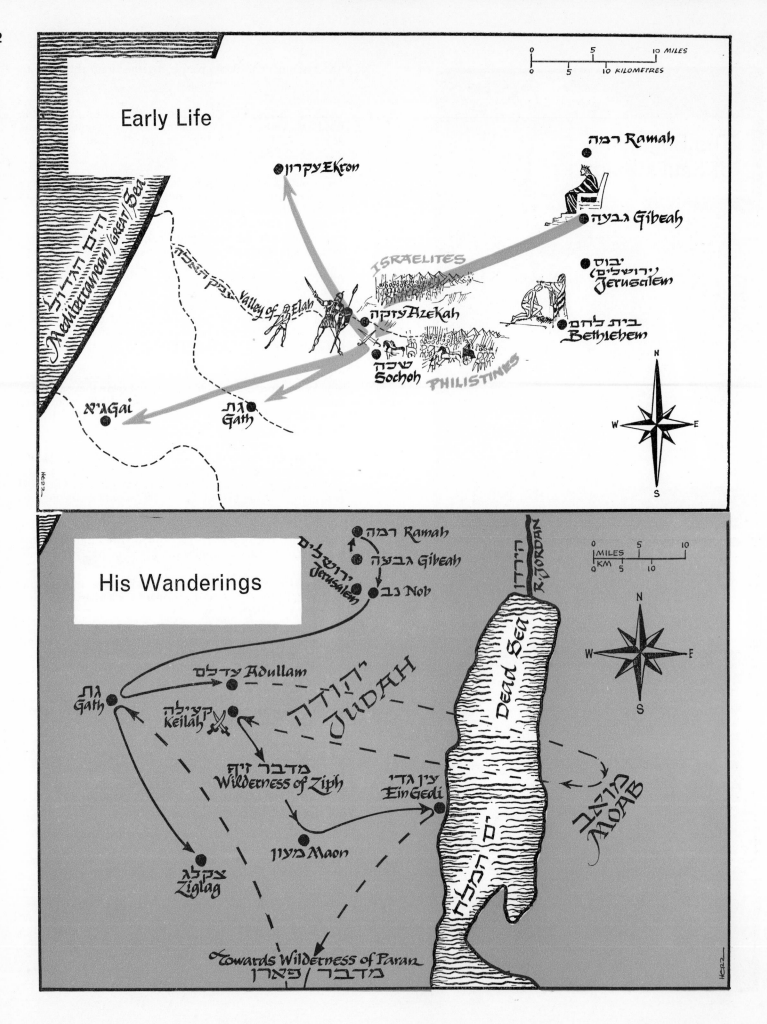

Early Life

Ramah רמה

Ekron עקרון

Gibeah גבעה

Jerusalem ירושלים/יבוס

Mediterranean/Great Sea הים הגדול

ISRAELITES

Valley of Elah עמק האלה

Azekah עזקה

Bethlehem בית לחם

Sochoh שכה

PHILISTINES

Gath גת

Gai גיא

His Wanderings

Ramah רמה

Gibeah גבעה

Jerusalem ירושלים

Nob נב

Adullam עדלם

Gath גת

Keilah קעילה

JUDAH יהודה

Wilderness of Ziph מדבר זיף

Ein Gedi עין גדי

Dead Sea ים המלח

R. Jordan הירדן

MOAB מואב

Ziglag צקלג

Maon מעון

Towards Wilderness of Paran מדבר/פארן

"And Samuel did that which the Lord spoke, and came to Bethlehem . . . Then Samuel took the horn of oil, and anointed him in the midst of his brethren; and the spirit of the Lord came mightily upon David from that day forward. So Samuel rose up, and went to Ramah." I Sam. 16 (4, 13).

"Now the Philistines gathered together their armies to battle, and they were gathered together at Sochoh which belongeth to Judah, and pitched between Sochoh and Azekah, in Ephes-dammim." I Sam. 17 (1).

"And Saul and the men of Israel were gathered together, and pitched in the vale of Elah, and set the battle in array against the Philistines. And the Philistines stood on the mountain on one side, and Israel stood on the mountain on the other side; and there was a valley between them." I Sam. 17 (2, 3).

"And David put his hand in his bag, and took thence a stone, and slung it, and smote the Philistine in his forehead; and the stone sank into his forehead, and he fell upon his face to the earth." I Sam. 17 (49).

"And the men of Israel and of Judah arose, and shouted, and pursued the Philistines, until thou camest to Gai, and to the gates of Ekron. And the wounded of the Philistines fell down by the way to Shaaraim, even unto Gath, and unto Ekron." I Sam. 17 (52).

"Now David fled, and escaped, and came to Samuel to Ramah, and told him all that Saul had done to him. And he and Samuel went and dwelt in Naioth." I Sam. 19 (18). "And David fled from Naioth in Ramah, and came and said before Jonathan: 'What have I done? What is mine iniquity? And what is my sin before thy father, that he seeketh my life?' " I Sam. 20 (1).

"Then came David to Nob to Ahimelech the priest, and Ahimelech came to meet David trembling, and said unto him: 'Why art thou alone and no man with thee?'." I Sam. 21 (2). AV:21 (1)

"And David arose, and fled that day for fear of Saul, and went to Achish the king of Gath." I Sam. 21 (11). AV:21 (10)

"David therefore departed thence, and escaped to the cave of Adullam; and when his brethren and all his father's house heard it, they went down thither to him." I Sam. 22 (1).

"And David went thence to Mizpah of Moab; and he said unto the king of Moab: 'Let my father and my mother, I pray thee, come forth, and be with you, till I know what God will do for me'." I Sam. 22 (3).

"And the prophet Gad said unto David: 'Abide not in the stronghold; depart, and get thee into the land of Judah'. Then David departed, and came to the forest of Hereth." I Sam. 22 (5).

"And David and his men went to Keilah, and fought with the Philistines, and brought away their cattle, and slew

them with a great slaughter. So David saved the inhabitants of Keilah." I Sam. 23 (5).

"Then David and his men, who were about six hundred, arose and departed out of Keilah, and went whithersoever they could go . . .". I Sam. 23 (13).

"And David abode in the wilderness in the strongholds, and remained in the hill-country in the wilderness of Ziph. And Saul sought him every day, but God delivered him not into his hand." I Sam. 23 (14).

"And they arose, and went to Ziph before Saul; but David and his men were in the wilderness of Maon, in the Aravah on the south of Jeshimon." I Sam. 23 (24).

"And David went up from thence, and dwelt in the strongholds of Ein-gedi." I Sam. 24 (1).

"And Samuel died; and all Israel gathered themselves together, and lamented him, and buried him in his house at Ramah. And David arose, and went down to the wilderness of Paran." I Sam. 25 (1).

"And David arose, and passed over, he and the six hundred men that were with him, unto Achish the son of Maoch, king of Gath. And David dwelt with Achish at Gath, he and his men, every man with his household, even David with his two wives, Ahinoam the Jezreelitess, and Abigail the Carmelitess, Nabal's wife." I Sam. 27 (2, 3).

"Then Achish gave him Ziklag that day, wherefore Ziklag belongeth unto the kings of Judah unto this day." I Sam. 27 (6).

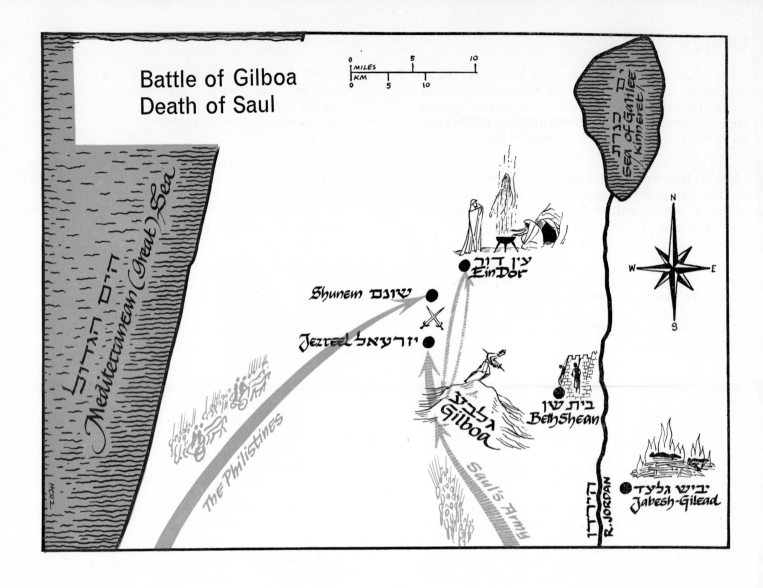

Battle of Gilboa
Death of Saul

"And the Philistines gathered themselves together, and came and pitched in Shunem; and Saul gathered all Israel together and they pitched in Gilboa." I Sam. 28 (4).

"Then said Saul unto his servants: 'Seek me a woman that divineth by a ghost, that I may go to her, and inquire of her'. And his servants said to him: 'Behold, there is a woman that divineth by a ghost at Ein-dor'." I Sam. 28 (7).

"Now the Philistines gathered together all their hosts to Aphek; and the Israelites pitched by the fountain which is in Jezreel." I Sam. 29 (1).

". . . And the Philistines went up to Jezreel." I Sam. 29 (11).

"Now the Philistines fought against Israel, and the men of

Israel fled from before the Philistines, and fell down slain in mount Gilboa." I Sam. 31 (1).

". . . therefore Saul took his sword and fell upon it." I Sam. 31 (4).

"And it came to pass on the morrow, when the Philistines came to strip the slain, that they found Saul and his three sons fallen in mount Gilboa . . . and they fastened his body to the wall of Beth-shean." I Sam. 31 (8, 10).

"And when the inhabitants of Jabesh-gilead heard concerning him that which the Philistines had done to Saul, all the valiant men arose, and went all night, and took the body of Saul and the bodies of his sons from the wall of Beth-shean; and they came to Jabesh, and burnt them there." I Sam. 31 (11, 12).

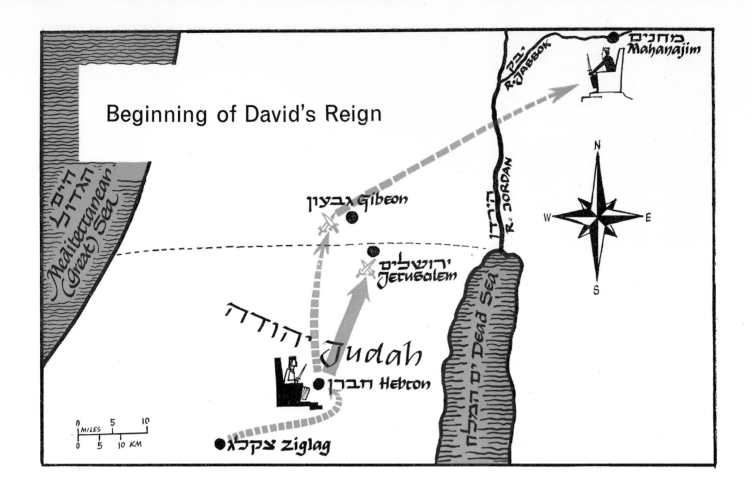

Beginning of David's Reign

"And it came to pass after the death of Saul, when David was returned from the slaughter of the Amalekites, and David had abode two days in Ziglag." II Sam. 1 (1).

"And his men that were with him did David bring up, every man with his household; and they dwelt in the cities of Hebron." II Sam. 2 (3).

"And the men of Judah came, and they anointed David king over the house of Judah." II Sam. 2 (4).

"Now Abner the son of Ner, captain of Saul's host, had taken Ish-bosheth the son of Saul, and brought him over to Mahanaim; and he made him king over Gilead, and over the Ashurites, and over Jezreel, and over Ephraim, and over Benjamin, and over all Israel." II Sam. 2 (8–9).

"And the time that David was king in Hebron over the house of Judah was seven years and six months." II Sam. 2 (11).

"And Abner the son of Ner, and the servants of Ish-bosheth the son of Saul, went out from Mahanaim to Gibeon. And Joab the son of Zeruiah, and the servants of David, went out; and they met together by the pool of Gibeon . . ." II Sam. 2 (12, 13).

"And Abner and his men went all that night through the Aravah; and they passed over the Jordan, and went through all Bithron, and came to Mahanaim." II Sam. 2 (29).

"So all the elders of Israel came to the king to Hebron; and king David made a covenant with them in Hebron before the Lord; and they anointed David king over Israel." II Sam. 5 (3).

"And the king and his men went to Jerusalem against the Jebusites . . ." II Sam. 5 (6).

"Nevertheless David took the stronghold of Zion, the same is the city of David." II Sam. 5 (7).

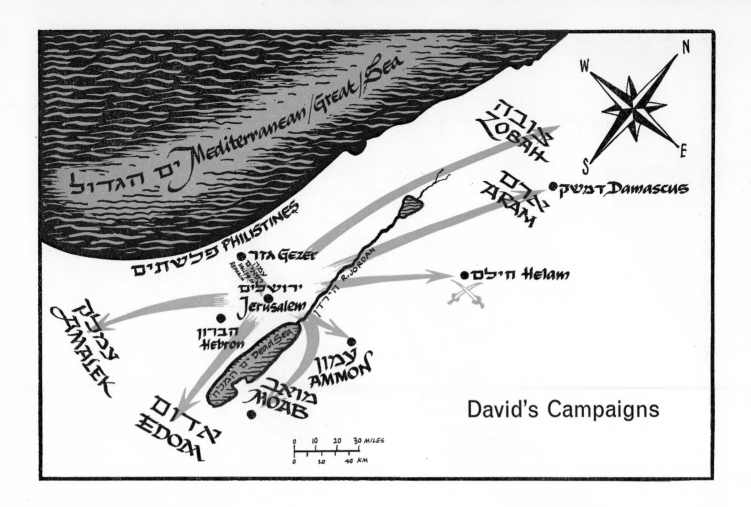

David's Campaigns

"Now the Philistines had come and spread themselves in the valley of Rephaim." II Sam. 5 (18).

"And David did so, as the Lord commanded him, and smote the Philistines from Geba until thou come to Gezer." II Sam. 5 (25).

"And after this it came to pass, that David smote the Philistines, and subdued them . . ." II Sam. 8 (1).

"And he smote Moab . . ." II Sam. 8 (2).

"David smote also Hadadezer the son of Rehob, king of Zobah, as he went to establish his dominion at the river Euphrates." II Sam. 8 (3).

"And . . . David smote of the Arameans two and twenty thousand men. Then David put garrisons in Aram of Damascus . . ." II Sam. 8 (5–6).
Note: Amalek is also mentioned among the nations subdued by David. See II Sam. 8 (12).

"And he put garrisons in Edom; throughout all Edom he put garrisons, and all the Edomites became servants to David. And the Lord gave victory to David whithersoever he went." II Sam. 8 (14).

"And when the children of Ammon saw that they were become odious to David, the children of Ammon sent and hired the Arameans of Beth-rehob, and the Arameans of Zobah, twenty thousand footmen, and the king of Maacah with a thousand men, and the men of Tob twelve thousand men. And when David heard of it, he sent Joab, and all the host of the mighty men." II Sam. 10 (6, 7).

"So Joab and the people that were with him drew nigh unto the battle against the Arameans; and they fled before him." II Sam. 10 (13).

"And Hadadezer sent, and brought out the Arameans that were beyond the River; and they came to Helam, with Shobach the captain of the host of Hadadezer at their head. And it was told David; and he gathered all Israel together, and passed over the Jordan, and came to Helam. And the Arameans set themselves in array against David, and fought with him." II Sam. 10 (16, 17).

"And the Arameans fled before Israel; and David slew of the Arameans seven hundred drivers of chariots, and forty thousand horsemen, and smote Shobach the captain of their host, so that he died there." II Sam. 10 (18).

"Now Joab fought against Rabbah of the children of Ammon, and took the royal city. II Sam. 12 (26).

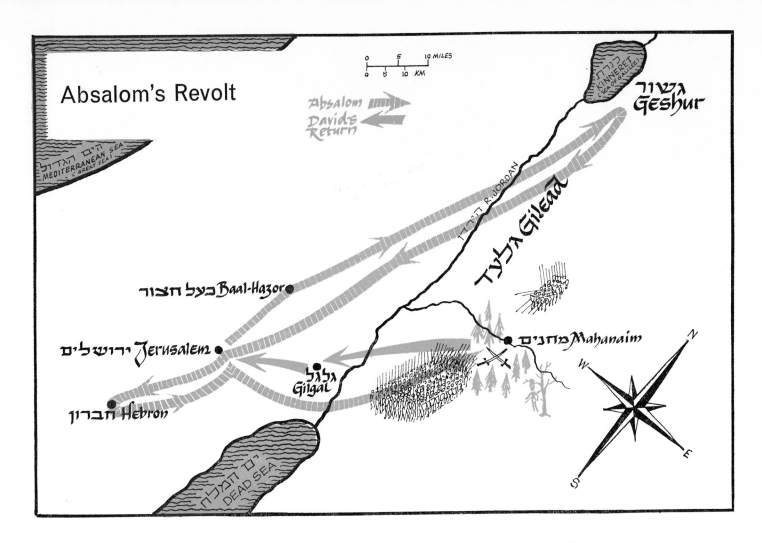

Absalom's Revolt

"And it came to pass after two full years, that Absalom had sheepshearers in Baal-hazor, which is beside Ephraim; and Absalom invited all the king's sons." II Sam. 13 (23).

"And it came to pass, while they were in the way, that the tidings came to David, saying: 'Absalom hath slain all the king's sons, and there is not one of them left'." II Sam. 13 (30).

"So Absalom fled, and went to Geshur, and was there three years." II Sam. 13 (38).

"So Joab arose and went to Geshur, and brought Absalom to Jerusalem." II Sam. 14 (23).

"And Absalom dwelt two full years in Jerusalem; and he saw not the king's face." II Sam. 14 (28).

"And it came to pass after this, that Absalom prepared him a chariot and horses, and fifty men to run before him." II Sam. 15 (1).

"And it came to pass at the end of forty years, that Absalom said unto the king: 'I pray thee, let me go and pay my vow, which I have vowed unto the Lord, in Hebron' . . . And the king said unto him: 'Go in peace'. So he arose, and went to Hebron." II Sam. 15 (7, 9).

"But Absalom sent spies throughout all the tribes of Israel, saying: 'As soon as ye hear the sound of the horn, then ye shall say: Absalom is king in Hebron'." II Sam. 15 (10).
Note: David's exact route of escape to Mahanaim cannot be identified with accuracy. See 15 (17, 23 and 30) and 16 (5).

"And Absalom, and all the people, the men of Israel, came to Jerusalem, and Ahithophel with him." II Sam. 16 (15).

"Then David arose, and all the people that were with him, and they passed over the Jordan; by the morning light there lacked not one of them that was not gone over the Jordan." II Sam. 17 (22).

"When David was come to Mahanaim, Absalom passed over the Jordan, he and all the men of Israel with him." II Sam. 17 (24).

"And Israel and Absalom pitched in the land of Gilead." II Sam. 17 (26).

"So the people went out into the field against Israel; and the battle was in the forest of Ephraim." II Sam. 18 (6).
Note: It has been suggested that the Tribe of Ephraim, located west of the Jordan (see page 20 "Division of the Land amongst the Tribes") had pasture rights east of the Jordan. Hence the woods there were called the "Forest of Ephraim".

"So the king returned, and came to the Jordan. And Judah came to Gilgal, to go to meet the king, to bring the king over the Jordan." II Sam. 19 (16). AV:19 (15)

"So the king went over to Gilgal . . ." II Sam. 19 (41). AV:19 (40)

"And David came to his house at Jerusalem' . . ." II Sam. 20 (3).

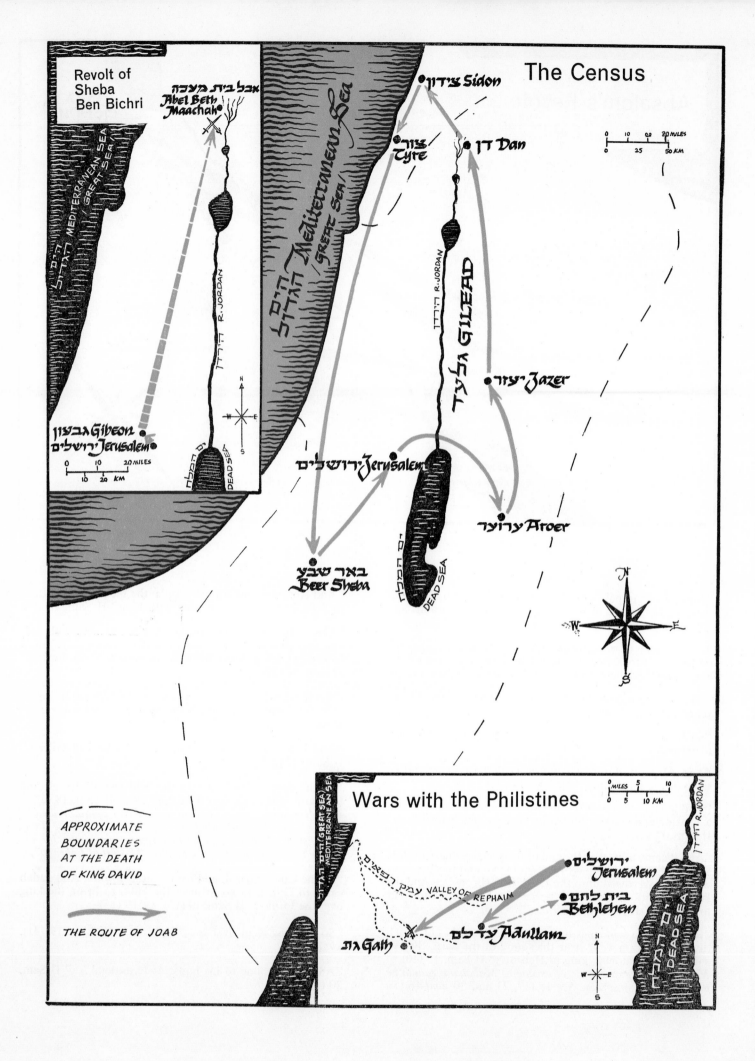

38

The Census

Revolt of
Sheba
Ben Bichri

אבל בית מעכה
Abel Beth
Maachah

MEDITERRANEAN SEA
GREAT SEA

הים התיכון Mediterranean Sea
GREAT SEA

צידון Sidon

צור Tyre

דן Dan

הירדן R.JORDAN

גלעד GILEAD

יעזר Jazer

ירושלים Jerusalem

ערוער Aroer

גבעון Gibeon
ירושלים Jerusalem

הים המלח DEAD SEA

באר שבע
Beer Sheba

הים המלח DEAD SEA

APPROXIMATE
BOUNDARIES
AT THE DEATH
OF KING DAVID

THE ROUTE OF JOAB

Wars with the Philistines

הים התיכון (GREAT SEA)
MEDITERRANEAN SEA

הירדן R.JORDAN

ירושלים
Jerusalem

עמק רפאים VALLEY OF REPHAIM

בית לחם
Bethlehem

עדלם Adullam

גת Gath

הים המלח DEAD SEA

Revolt of Sheba Ben Bichri

"Now there happened to be there a base fellow, whose name was Sheba, the son of Bichri, a Benjamite; and he blew the horn, and said: 'We have no portion in David, neither have we inheritance in the son of Jesse; every man to his tents, O Israel.' So all the men of Israel went up from following David, and followed Sheba the son of Bichri; but the men of Judah did cleave unto their king, from the Jordan even to Jerusalem." II Sam. 20 (1, 2).

"And there went out after him Joab's men, and the Cherethites and the Pelethites, and all the mighty men; and they went out of Jerusalem, to pursue after Sheba the son of Bichri." II Sam. 20 (7).

"When they were at the great stone which is in Gibeon, Amasa came to meet them . . ." II Sam. 20 (8).

"And he went through all the tribes of Israel unto Abel, and to Beth-maachah, . . ." II Sam. 20 (14).

". . . And they cut off the head of Sheba the son of Bichri, and threw it out to Joab. And he blew the horn, and they were dispersed from the city, every man to his tent. And Joab returned to Jerusalem unto the king." II Sam. 20 (22).

The Census

"And the king said to Joab the captain of the host that was with him: 'Go now to and fro through all the tribes of Israel, from Dan even to Beer-sheba, and number ye the people, that I may know the sum of the people'." II Sam. 24 (2).

"And they passed over the Jordan, and pitched in Aroer, on the right side of the city that is in the middle of the valley of Gad, and unto Jazer." II Sam. 24 (5).

"Then they came to Gilead, and to the land of Tahtim-hodshi; and they came to Dan-jaan, and round about to Sidon." II Sam. 24 (6).

"And they came to the stronghold of Tyre, and to all the cities of the Hivites, and of the Canaanites; and they went out to the south of Judah, at Beer-sheba." II Sam. 24 (7).

"So when they had gone to and fro through all the land, they came to Jerusalem at the end of the nine months and twenty days." II Sam. 24 (8).

Note: The census revealed a total of 1,300,000 men as inhabiting Israel and Judah, see II Sam. 24 (9). Of these, 70,000 died in the subsequent plague, see II Sam. 24 (15).

Wars with the Philistines

"And the Philistines had war again with Israel; and David went down, and his servants with him, and fought against the Philistines; and David waxed faint." II Sam. 21 (15).

"And it came to pass after this, that there was again war with the Philistines at Gob . . ." II Sam. 21 (18).

"And there was again war at Gath . . ." II Sam. 21 (20).

"And three of the thirty chiefs went down, and came to David in the harvest time unto the cave of Adullam; and the troop of the Philistines were encamped in the valley of Rephaim." II Sam. 23 (13).

"And David was then in the stronghold, and the garrison of the Philistines was then in Bethlehem. And David longed, and said: 'Oh that one would give me water to drink of the well of Bethlehem, which is by the gate!' And the three mighty men broke through the host of the Philistines, and drew water out of the well of Bethlehem, that was by the gate, and took it, and brought it to David; but he would not drink thereof, but poured it out unto the Lord." II Sam. 23 (14, 15, 16).

Note: The account in these chapters indicates that there was a number of incidents involving the Philistines. All the locations concerned cannot be identified with accuracy.

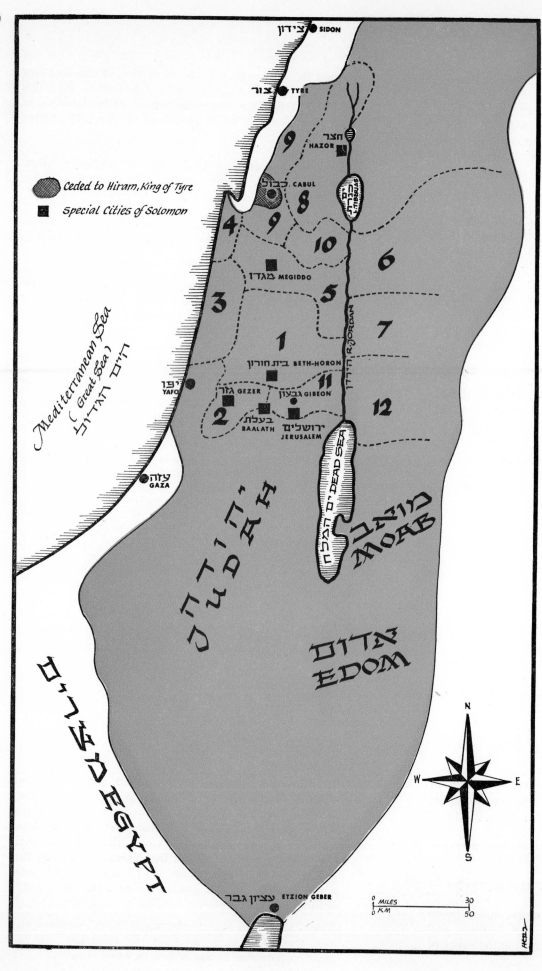

Ceded to Hiram, King of Tyre

Special Cities of Solomon

צידון SIDON

צור TYRE

חצר HAZOR

כבול CABUL

9

8

9

4

10

6

Mediterranean Sea
(Great Sea)
הים הגדול

מגדו MEGIDDO

3

5

7

1

ר׳ ירדן R. JORDAN

בית חורון BETH-HORON

יפו YAFO

גזר GEZER

גבעון GIBEON

11

2

בעלת BAALATH

ירושלים JERUSALEM

12

עזה GAZA

יהודה JUDAH

ים המלח DEAD SEA

מואב MOAB

אדום EDOM

מצרים EGYPT

עציון גבר ETZION GEBER

N

W   E

S

0   MILES   30
0   KM   50

Solomon

". . . and the kingdom was established in the hand of Solomon." I Kings 2 (46).

"And Solomon had twelve officers over all Israel, who provided victuals for the king and his household: each man to make provision for a month in the year." I Kings 4 (7).
Note: Details of the twelve districts and the names of the officers are contained in I Kings 4 (8–19).

"And Solomon ruled over all the kingdoms from the River unto the land of the Philistines, and unto the border of Egypt . . . For he had dominion over all the region on this side the river, from Tiphsah even to Gaza, over all the kings on this side the River; and he had peace on all sides round about him." I Kings 5 (1,4). AV:4 (21, 24)
Note: Details of the building of the temple are contained in I Kings 6 and 7.

"Then Solomon assembled the elders of Israel and all the heads of the tribes, the princes of the father's house and the children of Israel, unto King Solomon in Jerusalem, to bring up the ark of the covenant of the Lord out of the city of David, which is Zion." I Kings 8 (1).
Note: See "The Wandering of the Ark." p. 30.

"Now Hiram the King of Tyre had furnished Solomon with cedar trees and cypress trees, and with gold, according to all his desire—that then King Solomon gave Hiram twenty cities in the land of Galilee . . . and he called them the land of Cabul, unto this day." I Kings 9 (11, 13).

"And this is the account of the levy which King Solomon raised; to build the house of the Lord, and his own house, and Millo, and the wall of Jerusalem, and Hazor, and Megiddo, and Gezer . . . and Solomon built Gezer, and lower Beth-horon, and Baalath, and Tadmor in the wilderness, in the land, and all the store cities that Solomon had, and the cities for his chariots, and the cities for his horsemen . . . ." I Kings 9 (15, 17, 18, 19).
Note: Tadmor is not shown on the map but is generally identified with Palmyra, 200 miles North-East of Lake Kinneret.

"And King Solomon made a navy of ships in Etzion-geber, which is beside Eloth, on the shore of the Red Sea in the land Edom." I Kings 9 (26).

"For the king had at sea a navy of Tarshish with the navy of Hiram; once every three years came the navy of Tarshish, bringing gold and silver, ivory, and apes and peacocks." I Kings 10 (22).

42

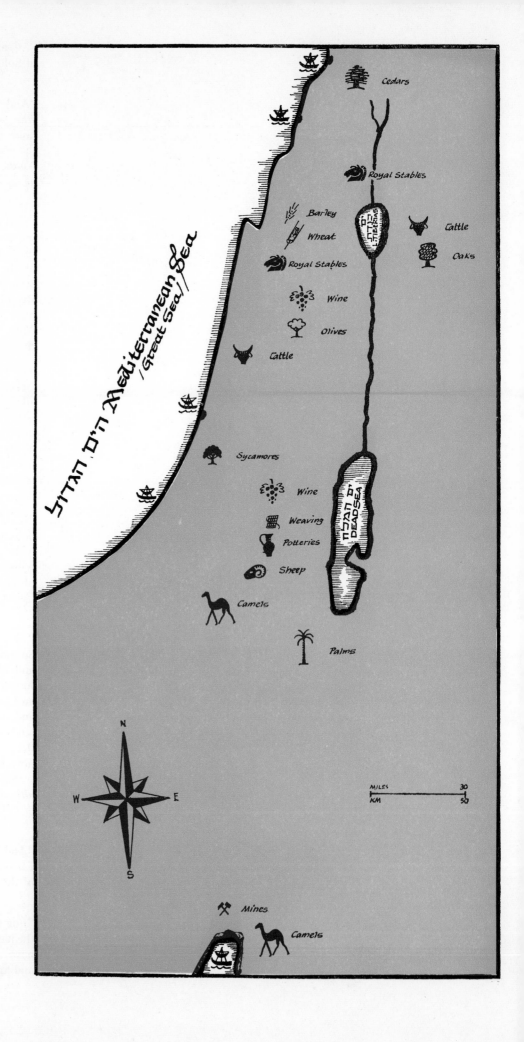

"For the Lord thy God bringeth thee into a good land, a land of brooks of water, of fountains and depths, that spring out in valleys and hills; a land of wheat and barley, and vines and fig-trees and pomegranates; a land of olive-trees and honey; a land wherein thou shalt eat bread without scarceness, thou shalt not lack any thing in it; a land whose stones are iron, and out of whose hills thou mayest dig brass." Deut. 8 (7–9).

"Judah and Israel were many, as the sand which is by the sea in multitude, eating and drinking and making merry." I Kings 4 (20).

"And Judah and Israel dwelt safely, every man under his vine and under his fig-tree, from Dan even to Beer-sheba, all the days of Solomon." I Kings 5 (5). AV:4 (25)

"And Solomon gave Hiram twenty thousand measures of wheat for food to his household, and twenty measures of beaten oil; thus gave Solomon to Hiram year by year." I Kings 5 (25). AV:5 (11)

"And Solomon gathered together chariots and horsemen; and he had a thousand and four hundred chariots, and twelve thousand horsemen, that he bestowed in the chariot cities and with the king at Jerusalem. And the king made silver to be in Jerusalem as stones, and cedars made he to be as the sycamore-trees that are in the Lowland, for abundance." I Kings 10 (26, 27).

"And all the kings of the earth sought the presence of Solomon, to hear his wisdom, which God had put in his heart. And they brought every man his present, vessels of silver and vessels of gold, and raiment, armour, and spices, horses and mules, a rate year by year." II Chron. 9 (23–24).
Note: See also II Chron. 9 (25–27).

"And they brought horses for Solomon out of Egypt and out of all lands." II Chron. 9 (28).
Note: See also I Chron. 4 (21–23) and I Chron. 27 (25–31).

44

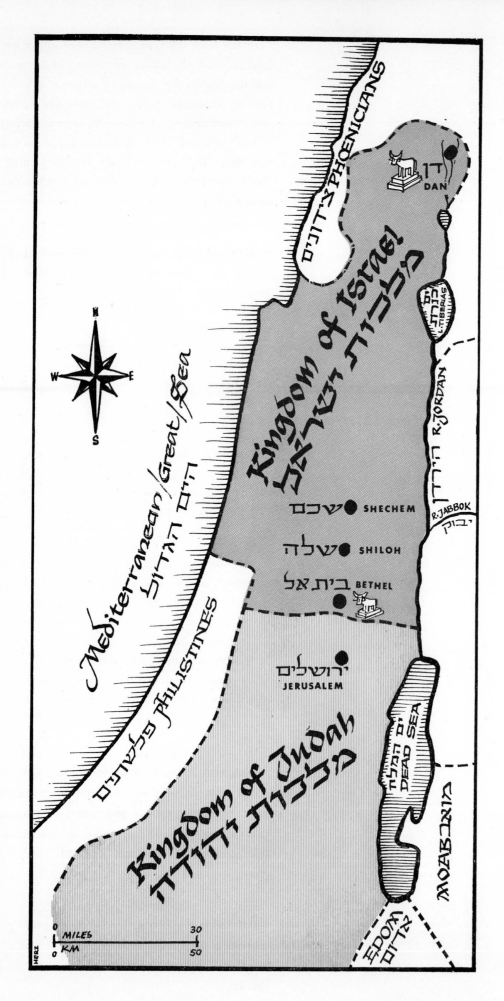

Division
of the
Kingdom

"And the time that Solomon reigned in Jerusalem over all Israel was forty years. And Solomon slept with his fathers, and was buried in the city of David his father; and Rehoboam his son reigned in his stead." I Kings 11 (42, 43).

"And Rehoboam went to Shechem; for all Israel came to Shechem to make him king." I Kings 12 (1).

"And when all Israel saw that the king hearkened not unto them, the people answered the king saying: 'What portion have we in David? Neither have we inheritance in the son of Jesse; to your tents, O Israel; now see to thine own house, David'. So Israel departed unto their tents. But as for the children of Israel that dwelt in the cities of Judah, Rehoboam reigned over them . . . So Israel rebelled against the house of David, unto this day." I Kings 12 (16, 17, 19).

"And it came to pass, when all Israel heard that Jeroboam was returned, that they sent and called him into the congregation, and made him king over all Israel; there was none that followed the house of David, but the tribe of Judah only." I Kings 12 (20).

"Then Jeroboam built Shechem in the hill country of Ephraim, and dwelt therein; . . ." I Kings 12 (25).

"Whereupon the king took counsel, and made two calves of gold . . . and he set the one in Beth-el and the other put he in Dan." I Kings 12 (28, 29).

"And it came to pass in the fifth year of King Rehoboam that Shishak King of Egypt came up against Jerusalem." I Kings 14 (25).

bijah

. And there was war between Abijah and Jeroboam." II Chron.
(2).

te: Abijah is called Abijam in I Kings 15.
te: The full account of the battle is contained in II Chron. 13.

nd Abijah pursued after Jeroboam and took cities from him,
h-el with the towns thereof, and Jeshanah with the towns thereof,
I Ephron with the towns thereof." II Chron. 13 (19).

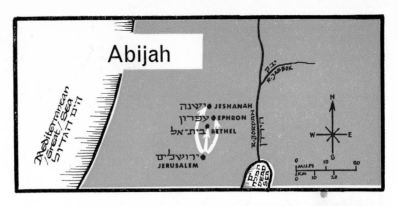

aasha and Asa and First Syrian
ampaign

nd Baasha the son of Ahijah, of the house of Issachar, conspired
inst him; (Nadab, son of Jeroboam) and Baasha smote him at
bbethon, which belonged to the Philistines; for Nadab and all
ael were laying siege to Gibbethon." I Kings 15 (27).

nd Baasha king of Israel went up against Judah, and built Ramah,
at he might not suffer any to go out or come in to Asa king of
lah." I Kings 15 (17).

hen Asa took all the silver and the gold that were left in the
asures of the house of the Lord, and the treasures of the king's
use, and delivered them into the hand of his servants; and king
a sent them to Ben-hadad, the son of Tabrimmon, the son of
zion, king of Syria that dwelt at Damascus . . ." I Kings 15 (18).

nd Ben-hadad hearkened unto king Asa, and sent the captains
his armies against the cities of Israel, and smote Ijon, and Dan,
d Abel-beth-maachah, and all Chinneroth, with all the land of
phtali." I Kings 15 (20).

nd it came to pass, when Baasha heard thereof, that he left off
ilding Ramah, and dwelt in Tirzah." I Kings 15 (21).

hen king Asa made a proclamation unto all Judah; none was
empted; and they carried away the stones of Ramah, and the
mber thereof, wherewith Baasha had builded; and king Asa built
erewith Geba of Benjamin, and Mizpah." I Kings 15 (22).

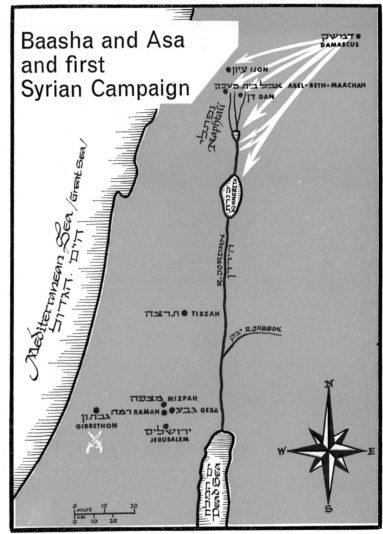

imri   Omri

the twenty and seventh year of Asa king of Judah did Zimri
gn seven days in Tirzah. Now the people were encamped against
bbethon, which belonged to the Philistines." I Kings 16 (15).
nd the people that were encamped heard say: 'Zimri hath con-
red (against Elah son of Baasha), and hath also smitten the king';
erefore all Israel made Omri, the captain of the host, king over
ael that day in the camp." I Kings 16 (16).
nd Omri went up from Gibbethon, and all Israel with him, and
y besieged Tirzah." I Kings 16 (17).

nd it came to pass, when Zimri saw that the city was taken, that
went into the castle of the king's house, and burnt the king's
use over himself with fire and died." I Kings 16 (18).
hen were the people of Israel divided into two parts: half of the
ople followed Tibni the son of Ginath, to make him king, and
lf followed Omri. But the people that followed Omri prevailed . . .
Tibni died, and Omri reigned." I Kings 16 (21, 22).
the thirty and first year of Asa king of Judah began Omri to
gn over Israel and reigned twelve years; six years reigned he in
zah." I Kings 16 (23).

nd he bought the hill Samaria . . . and called the name of the city
ich he built Samaria . . ." I Kings 16 (24).
te: The Capital of the Northern Kingdom henceforth was at
maria.

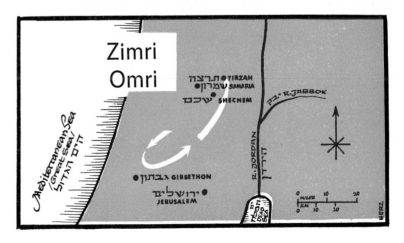

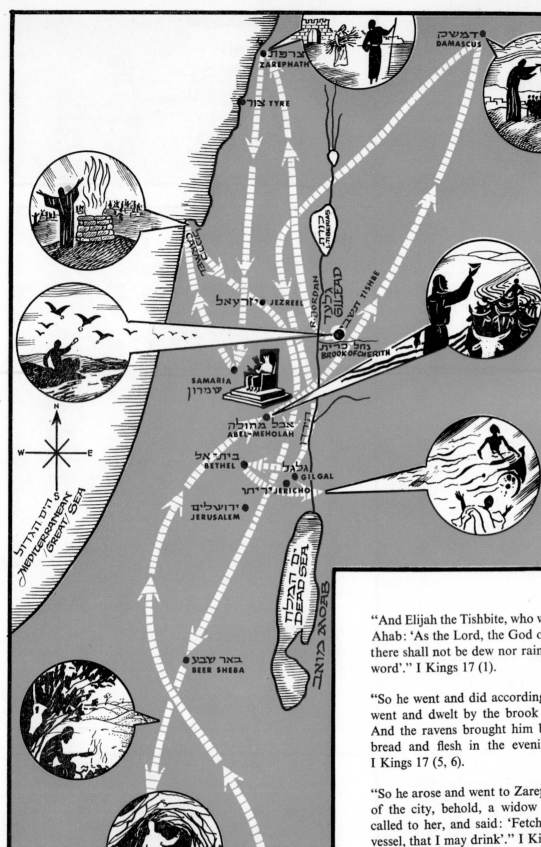

"And Elijah the Tishbite, who was of the settlers of Gilead, said unto Ahab: 'As the Lord, the God of Israel, liveth, before whom I stand, there shall not be dew nor rain in these years, but according to my word'." I Kings 17 (1).

"So he went and did according unto the word of the Lord; for he went and dwelt by the brook Cherith, that is before the Jordan. And the ravens brought him bread and flesh in the morning and bread and flesh in the evening; and he drank of the brook." I Kings 17 (5, 6).

"So he arose and went to Zarephath, and when he came to the gate of the city, behold, a widow was there gathering sticks; and he called to her, and said: 'Fetch me, I pray thee, a little water in a vessel, that I may drink'." I Kings 17 (10).

Note: Zarephath was the scene of the miracles of the meal and oil that was not spent and the son who was revived. See I Kings 17 (11–24).

"And it came to pass after many days, that the word of the Lord came to Elijah, in the third year, saying: 'Go, show thyself unto Ahab, and I will send rain upon the land'." I Kings 18 (1).

"'Now therefore send, and gather to me all Israel unto Mount Carmel, and the prophets of Baal four hundred and fifty, and the prophets of the Asherah four hundred that eat at Jezebel's table'." I Kings 18 (19).
Note: The encounter of Elijah and the false prophets on Mount Carmel is told in I Kings 18 (20–45).

"And the hand of the Lord was on Elijah; and he girded up his loins, and ran before Ahab to the entrance of Jezreel." I Kings 18 (46).

"And he arose, and went for his life, and came to Beer-sheba, which belongeth to Judah, and left his servant there." I Kings 19 (3).

"But he himself went a day's journey into the wilderness, and came and sat down under a juniper tree; and he requested for himself that he might die; and said: 'It is enough; now, O Lord, take away my life; for I am not better than my fathers.'" I Kings 19 (4).

"And he arose, and did eat and drink, and went in the strength of that meal forty days and forty nights unto Horeb the mount of God." I Kings 19 (8).

"And the Lord said unto him: 'Go return on thy way to the wilderness of Damascus; and when thou comest, thou shalt anoint Hazael to be king over Syria and Jehu the son of Nimshi shalt thou anoint to be king over Israel; and Elisha the son of Shaphat of Abel-meholah shalt thou anoint to be prophet in thy stead'." I Kings 19 (15, 16).

"So he departed thence and found Elisha the son of Shaphat who was plowing with twelve yoke of oxen before him . . ." I Kings 19 (19).

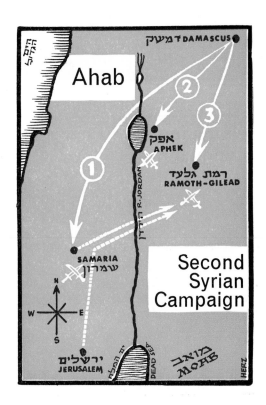

"'Arise, go down to meet Ahab king of Israel, who dwelleth in Samaria; behold, he is in the vineyard of Naboth, whither he is gone down to take possession of it.'" I Kings 21 (18).
Note: See II Kings 1 (2–17) for the incident involving Elijah and Ahaziah, son of Ahab, king of Israel.

"And it came to pass when the Lord would take up Elijah by a whirlwind into Heaven, that Elijah went with Elisha from Gilgal. And Elijah said unto Elisha: 'Tarry here, I pray thee, for the Lord hath sent me as far as Beth-el'. . . ." II Kings 2 (1, 2).

"And Elijah said unto him: 'Elisha, tarry here, I pray thee; for the Lord hath sent me to Jericho'. . . ." II Kings 2 (4).

"And Elijah said unto him: 'Tarry here, I pray thee; for the Lord hath sent me to the Jordan'. . . ." II Kings 2 (6).

"And fifty men of the sons of the prophets went, and stood over against them afar off; and they two stood by the Jordan. And Elijah took his mantle, and wrapped it together, and smote the waters, and they were divided hither and thither, so that they two went over on dry ground." II Kings 2 (7, 8).

"And it came to pass, as they still went on, and talked, that, behold, there appeared a chariot of fire, and horses of fire, which parted them both asunder; and Elijah went up by a whirlwind unto Heaven." II Kings 2 (11).
Note: The route of Elijah, shown on the map, is intended as a general, approximate guide.

Ahab   Second Syrian Campaign

"And Ben-hadad the king of Syria gathered all his host together; and there were thirty and two kings with him, and horses and chariots; and he went up and besieged Samaria, and fought against it." I Kings 20 (1).

"And it came to pass at the return of the year, that Ben-hadad mustered the Syrians and went up to Aphek, to fight against Israel." I Kings 20 (26).
Note: The account of this, the second battle of the campaign, is contained in I Kings 20 (26–43).

"And there continued three years without war between Syria and Israel. And it came to pass in the third year, that Jehoshaphat the king of Judah came down to the King of Israel." I Kings 22 (1, 2).

"So the king of Israel and Jehoshaphat the king of Judah went up to Ramoth-gilead." I Kings 22 (29).

"So the king (Ahab) died, and was brought to Samaria; and they buried the king in Samaria." I Kings 22 (37).

"And Moab rebelled against Israel after the death of Ahab." II Kings 1 (1).

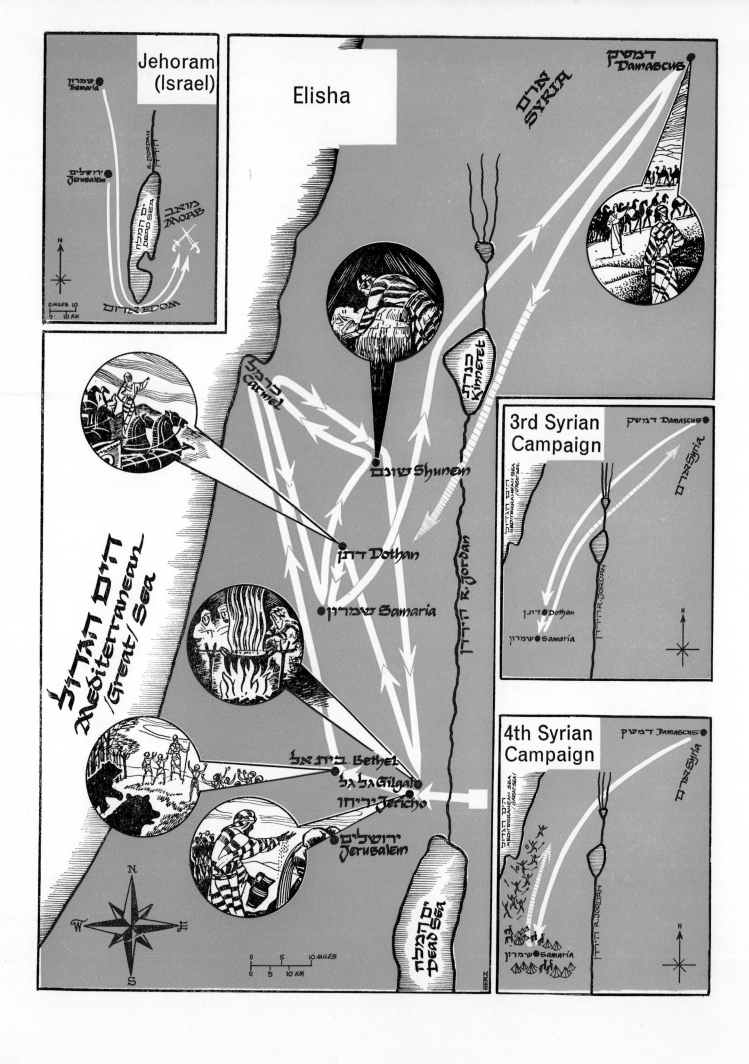

48

Jehoram
(Israel)

Elisha

3rd Syrian
Campaign

4th Syrian
Campaign

Jehoram (Israel)

Elisha

*Note: See page 47 "Elijah"—for the anointing of Elisha and *his journey, with Elijah, to the Jordan.* "And when the sons of the prophets that were at Jericho some way off saw him, they said: 'The spirit of Elijah doth rest on Elisha.' And they came to meet him, and bowed down to the ground before him." II Kings 2 (15).

Note: II Kings 2 (19–22) describes the healing of the waters of Jericho by Elisha.

"And he went up from thence unto Beth-el; and as he was going up by the way, there came forth little children out of the city, and mocked him, and said unto him: 'Go up, thou baldhead; go up, thou baldhead.' And he looked before him and saw them, and cursed them in the name of the Lord. And there came forth two she-bears out of the wood, and tore forty and two children of them." II Kings 2 (23, 24).

"And he went from thence to Mount Carmel, and from thence he returned to Samaria." II Kings 2 (25).

"And it fell on a day, that Elisha passed to Shunem, where was a great woman; and she constrained him to eat bread. And so it was, that as oft as he passed by, he turned in thither to eat bread." II Kings 4 (8).

Note: Elisha frequently travelled between Samaria and Carmel via Shunem. For the story of Elisha and the child of the Shunemmite see II Kings 4 (8–37).

"And Elisha came again to Gilgal and there was a famine in the land; and the sons of the prophets were sitting before him; and he said unto his servant: 'Set on the great pot, and seethe pottage for the sons of the prophets'." II Kings 4 (38).

Note: For the story of Elisha and the healing of Naaman, the Syrian Army Commander, see II Kings 5.

"Now Jehoram the son of Ahab began to reign over Israel in Samaria. . . ." II Kings 3 (1).

"Now the king of Syria warred against Israel. . . ." II Kings 6 (8). *Note: See Map "3rd Syrian Campaign". See II Kings 6 (8-23).*

Note: Elisha was staying at Dothan, see II Kings 6 (13), and subsequently went to Samaria, see II Kings 6 (19).

"But it came to pass, when Ahab was dead, that (Mesha) the king of Moab rebelled against the king of Israel." II Kings 3 (5).

"And it came to pass after this, that Ben-hadad king of Syria gathered all his host, and went up, and besieged Samaria." II Kings 6 (24). *Note: See Map "4th Syrian Campaign". See II Kings 6 (24), II Kings 7 (20).*

Note: See II Kings 8 (1–6) for a further incident involving the Shunemmite woman.

"And he (Jehoram) went and sent to Jehoshaphat the king of Judah, saying: 'The king of Moab hath rebelled against me; wilt thou go with me against Moab to battle?' And he said: 'I will go up; I am as thou art, my people as thy people, my horses as thy horses'." II Kings 3 (7).

"And Elisha came to Damascus; and Ben-hadad the king of Syria was sick; and it was told him, saying: 'The man of God is come hither'." II Kings 8 (7).

Note: See II Kings 8 (7–15) for the full account of Elisha's encounter with Hazael.

Note: For Elisha's instructions regarding the anointing of Jehu, see page 50 "Jehu".

"And he said: 'Which way shall we go up?' And he answered: 'The way of the wilderness of Edom'. So the king of Israel went, and the king of Judah, and the king of Edom; and they made a circuit of seven days' journey; and there was no water for the host, nor for the beasts that followed them." II Kings 3 (8, 9).

"And Elisha died, and they buried him. . . ." II Kings 13 (20). *Note: The route of Elisha, shown on the map, is intended as a general, approximate guide.*

"Now when all the Moabites heard that the kings were come up to fight against them, they gathered themselves together, all that were able to put on armour, and upward, and stood on the border." II Kings 3 (21).

"And when they came to the camp of Israel, the Israelites rose up and smote the Moabites, so that they fled before them. And they smote the land, even Moab, mightily." II Kings 3 (24).

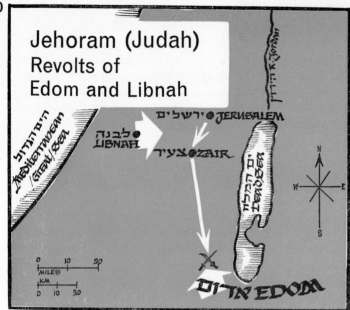

Jehoram (Judah)

Note: The name "Jehoram", borne by both a king of Israel and a king of Judah, also appears in the contracted form of "Joram".

"And in the fifth year of Joram the son of Ahab king of Israel, Jehoshaphat being then king of Judah, Jehoram the son of Jehoshaphat king of Judah began to reign." II Kings 8 (16).

"In his days Edom revolted from under the hand of Judah, and made a king over themselves." II Kings 8 (20).

"Then Joram (*King of Judah*) passed over to Zair, and all his chariots with him; and he rose up by night, and smote the Edomites that compassed him about, and the captains of the chariots; and the people fled to their tents." II Kings 8 (21).

"Yet Edom revolted from under the hand of Judah, unto this day. Then did Libnah revolt at the same time." II Kings 8 (22).

Jehoram (Israel)   Ahaziah (Judah)

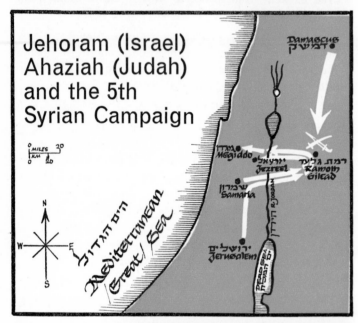

"In the twelfth year of Joram the son of Ahab king of Israel did Ahaziah the son of Jehoram king of Judah begin to reign." II Kings 8 (25).

"And he (*Ahaziah*) went with Joram the son of Ahab to war against Hazael king of Syria at Ramoth-gilead; and the Syrians wounded Joram." II Kings 8 (28).

"And king Joram returned to be healed in Jezreel of the wounds which the Syrians had given him at Ramah (*i.e. Ramoth-gilead*), when he fought against Hazael king of Syria. And Ahaziah the son of Jehoram king of Judah went down to see Joram the son of Ahab in Jezreel, because he was sick." II Kings 8 (29).

Note: The subsequent story of Jehoram and Ahaziah is contained in the account of Jehu.

Jehu

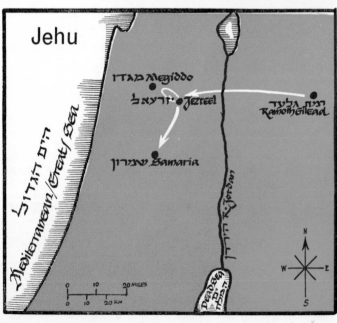

"And Elisha the prophet called one of the sons of the prophets, and said unto him: 'Gird up thy loins, and take this vial of oil in thy hands, and go to Ramoth-gilead. And when thou comest thither, look out there Jehu the son of Jehoshaphat the son of Nimshi, and go in, and make him arise up from among his brethren, and carry him to an inner chamber. Then take the vial of oil, and pour it on his head, and say: Thus saith the Lord: I have anointed thee king over Israel. Then open the door, and flee, and tarry not'." II Kings 9 (1, 2, 3).

"Jehu the son of Jehoshaphat conspired against Joram." II Kings 9 (14).

"So Jehu rode in a chariot, and went to Jezreel; for Joram lay there. And Ahaziah king of Judah was come to see Joram." II Kings 9 (16).

"And Joram said: 'Make ready'. And they made ready his chariot. And Joram king of Israel and Ahaziah king of Judah went out, each in his chariot, and they went out to meet Jehu, and found him in the portion of Naboth the Jezreelite." II Kings 9 (21).

"And Jehu drew his bow with his full strength, and smote Joram between his arms, and the arrow went out at his heart, and he sunk down in his chariot." II Kings 9 (24).

"But when Ahaziah the king of Judah saw this, he fled by the way of the garden-house. And Jehu followed after him, and said: 'Smite him also in the chariot'; (and they did so) at the ascent of Gur, which is by Ibleam. And he fled to Megiddo, and died there. And his servants carried him in a chariot to Jerusalem, and buried him . . . in the city of David." II Kings 9 (27, 28).

"And when Jehu was come to Jezreel, Jezebel (*wife of Ahab and mother of Jehoram of Israel*) heard of it; and she painted her eyes, and attired her head, and looked out at the window." II Kings 9 (30).

Note: The death of Jezebel is described in verses 31–37.

"And he (*Jehu*) arose and departed, and went to Samaria . . ." II Kings 10 (12).

"And when he came to Samaria, he smote all that remained unto Ahab in Samaria, till he had destroyed him, according to the word of the Lord, which he spoke to Elijah." II Kings 10 (17).

"And Jehu slept with his fathers; and they buried him in Samaria. And Jehoahaz his son reigned in his stead." II Kings 10 (35).

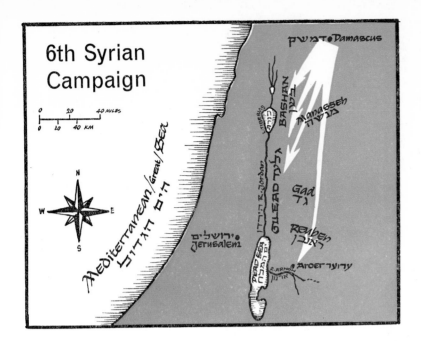

6th Syrian Campaign

"In those days the Lord began to cut Israel short; and Hazael smote them in all the borders of Israel: from the Jordan eastward, all the land of Gilead, the Gadites, and the Reubenites, and the Manassites, from Aroer, which is by the valley of Arnon, even Gilead and Bashan." II Kings 10 (32, 33).

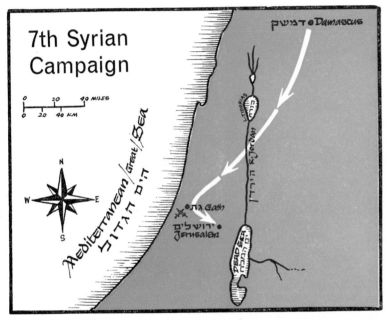

7th Syrian Campaign

"Then Hazael king of Syria went up, and fought against Gath, and took it; and Hazael set his face to go up to Jerusalem. And Jehoash king of Judah took all the hallowed things that Jehoshaphat, and Jehoram, and Ahaziah, his fathers, kings of Judah, had dedicated, and his own hallowed things, and all the gold that was found in the treasures of the house of the Lord, and of the king's house, and sent it to Hazael king of Syria; and he went away from Jerusalem." II Kings 12 (18, 19). AV:12 (17, 18)

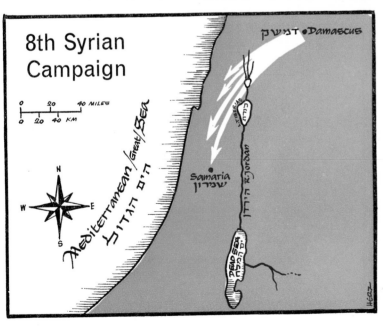

8th Syrian Campaign

"In the three and twentieth year of Joash the son of Ahaziah, king of Judah, Jehoahaz the son of Jehu began to reign over Israel in Samaria, and reigned seventeen years." II Kings 13 (1).

"And the anger of the Lord was kindled against Israel, and He delivered them into the hand of Hazael king of Syria, and the hand of Ben-hadad the son of Hazael, all their days." II Kings 13 (3).

"And Jehoahaz besought the Lord, and the Lord hearkened unto him, for He saw the oppression of Israel, how that the king of Syria oppressed them." II Kings 13 (4).

"And the Lord gave Israel a deliverer, so that they went out from under the hand of the Syrians, and the children of Israel dwelt in their tents as beforetime." II Kings 13 (5).

"For there was not left to Jehoahaz of the people save fifty horsemen, and ten chariots, and ten thousand footmen; for the king of Syria destroyed them, and made them like the dust in threshing." II Kings 13 (7).

"And Hazael king of Syria oppressed Israel all the days of Jehoahaz." II Kings 13 (22).

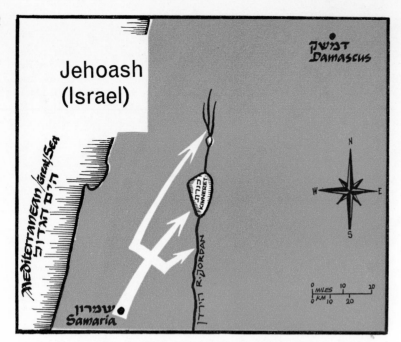

Jehoash (Israel)

Note: The name "Jehoash", borne by both a king of Israel and a king of Judah, also appears in the contracted form of "Joash."

"In the thirty and seventh year of Joash king of Judah began Jehoash the son of Jehoahaz to reign over Israel in Samaria, and reigned sixteen years." II Kings 13 (10).

"And Hazael king of Syria died; and Ben-hadad his son reigned in his stead." II Kings 13 (24).

"And Jehoash the son of Jehoahaz took again out of the hand of Ben-hadad the son of Hazael the cities which he had taken out of the hand of Jehoahaz his father by war. Three times did Joash smite him, and recovered the cities of Israel." II Kings 13 (25).

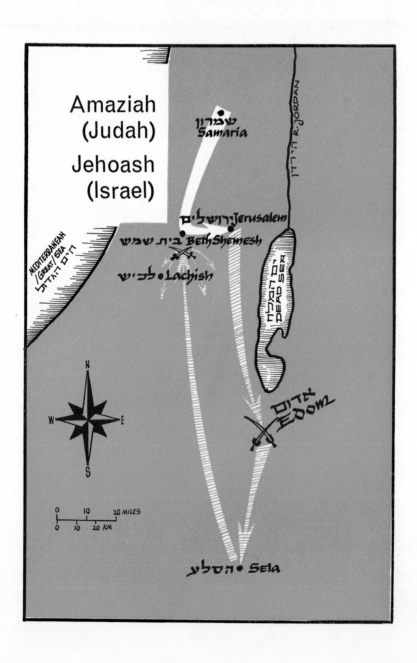

Amaziah (Judah)   Jehoash (Israel)

"In the second year of Joash son of Joahaz king of Israel began Amaziah the son of Joash king of Judah to reign." II Kings 14 (1).

"He slew of Edom in the Valley of Salt ten thousand, and took Sela by war, and called the name of it Joktheel, unto this day." II Kings 14 (7).
Note: Sela was also known as Petra, the name it bears today.

"Then Amaziah sent messengers to Jehoash, the son of Jehoahaz son of Jehu, king of Israel, saying: 'Come, let us look one another in the face'." II Kings 14 (8).

". . . So Jehoash king of Israel went up; and he and Amaziah king of Judah looked one another in the face at Beth-shemesh, which belongeth to Judah. And Judah was put to the worse before Israel; and they fled every man to his tent." II Kings 14 (11, 12).

"And Jehoash king of Israel took Amaziah king of Judah, the son of Jehoash the son of Ahaziah, at Beth-shemesh, and came to Jerusalem, and broke down the wall of Jerusalem from the gate of Ephraim unto the corner gate, four hundred cubits." II Kings 14 (13).

"And he took all the gold and silver, and all the vessels that were found in the house of the Lord, and in the treasures of the king's house, the hostages also, and returned to Samaria." II Kings 14 (14).

"And they made a conspiracy against him (*Amaziah*) in Jerusalem; and he fled to Lachish; but they sent after him to Lachish, and slew him there. And they brought him upon horses; and he was buried at Jerusalem with his fathers in the city of David." II Kings 14 (19, 20).

Jeroboam II

"In the fifteenth year of Amaziah the son of Joash king of Judah, Jeroboam the son of Joash king of Israel began to reign in Samaria, and reigned forty and one years." II Kings 14 (23).

"He restored the border of Israel from the Entrance to Hamath unto the sea of Aravah, according to the word of the Lord, the God of Israel, which He spoke by the hand of His servant Jonah the son of Amittai, the prophet, who was of Gath-hepher." II Kings 14 (25).

"Now the rest of the acts of Jeroboam, and all that he did, and his might, how he warred, and how he recovered Damascus, and Hamath, for Judah in Israel, are they not written in the book of the chronicles of the kings of Israel?" II Kings 14 (28).

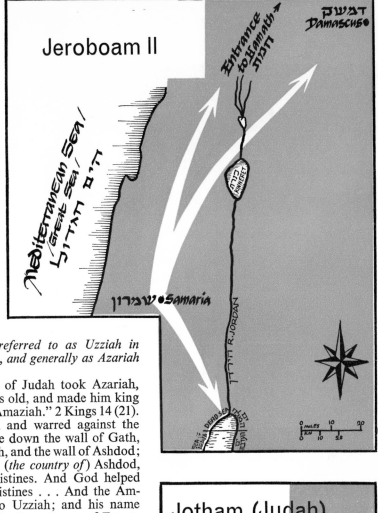

Uzziah (Azariah)

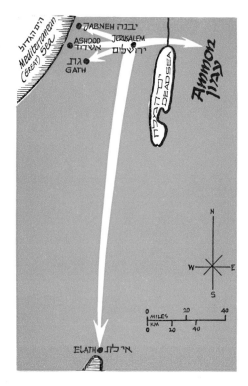

Note: This king is referred to as Uzziah in Chronicles and Isaiah, and generally as Azariah in the Book of Kings.

"And all the people of Judah took Azariah, who was sixteen years old, and made him king instead of his father Amaziah." 2 Kings 14 (21).

"And he went forth and warred against the Philistines, and broke down the wall of Gath, and the wall of Jabneh, and the wall of Ashdod; and he built cities in (*the country of*) Ashdod, and among the Philistines. And God helped him against the Philistines . . . And the Ammonites gave gifts to Uzziah; and his name spread abroad even to the entrance of Egypt; for he waxed exceeding strong." II Chronicles 26 (6, 7, 8).

"Moreover Uzziah built towers in Jerusalem at the corner gate, and at the valley gate, and at the Turning of the Wall and fortified them. And he built towers in the wilderness, and hewed out many cisterns, for he had much cattle; in the Lowland also, and in the plain, and he had husbandmen and vinedressers in the mountains and in the fruitful fields; for he loved husbandry." 2 Chronicles 26 (9, 10).

"He built Elath, and restored it to Judah. . . ." II Kings 14 (22).

"And Azariah slept with his fathers and they buried him with his fathers in the City of David and his son Jotham reigned in his stead." II Kings 15 (7).

Jotham (Judah) and the 9th Syrian Campaign

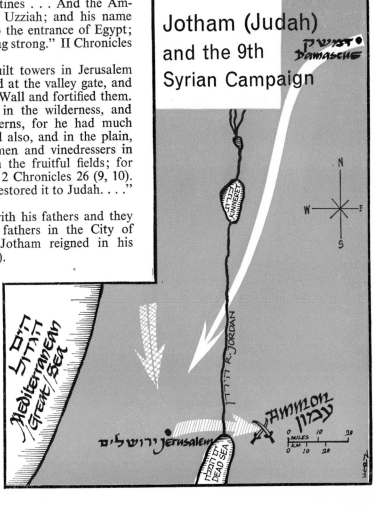

Jotham (Judah)

"In the second year of Pekah the son of Remaliah king of Israel began Jotham the son of Uzziah king of Judah to reign." II Kings 15 (32).

"He fought also with the king of the children of Ammon, and prevailed against them. And the children of Ammon gave him the same year a hundred talents of silver, and ten thousand measures of wheat, and ten thousand of barley. So much did the children of Ammon render unto him, in the second year also, and in the third." II Chronicles 27 (5).

"In those days the Lord began to send against Judah Rezin the king of Syria, and Pekah the son of Remaliah." II Kings 15 (37).

Menahem (Israel) First Assyrian Attack

"And Menahem the son of Gadi went up from Tirzah, and came to Samaria, and smote Shallum the son of Jabesh in Samaria, and slew him, and reigned in his stead." II Kings 15 (14).

"Then Menahem smote Tiphsah, and all that were therein, and the borders thereof, from Tirzah; because they opened not to him, therefore he smote it; and all the women therein that were with child he ripped up." II Kings 15 (16).

"There came against the land Pul the king of Assyria; and Menahem gave Pul a thousand talents of silver, that his hand might be with him to confirm the kingdom in his hand. . . . So the king of Assyria turned back, and stayed not there in the land." II Kings 15 (19, 20).

"And Menahem slept with his fathers; and Pekahiah his son reigned in his stead." II Kings 15 (22).

Pekah (Israel)—Second Assyrian Attack

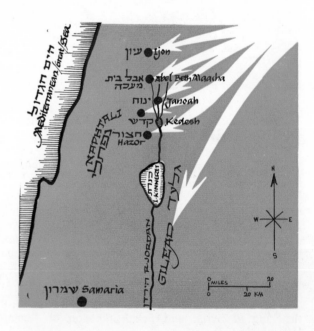

"And Pekah the son of Remaliah, his captain, conspired against him (*Pekahiah*), and smote him in Samaria, in the castle of the king's house, by Argob and by Arieh; and with him were fifty men of the Gileadites; and he slew him, and reigned in his stead. In the fifty-second year of Azariah king of Judah, Pekah the son of Remaliah began to reign over Israel in Samaria, and reigned twenty years." II Kings 15 (25, 27).

"In the days of Pekah king of Israel came Tiglath-pileser king of Assyria, and took Ijon, and Abel-beth-maachah, and Janoah, and Kedesh, and Hazor, and Gilead, and Galilee, all the land of Naphtali; and he carried them captive to Assyria." II Kings 15 (29).

"And Hoshea the son of Elah made a conspiracy against Pekah the son of Remaliah, and smote him, and slew him, and reigned in his stead, in the twentieth year of Jotham the son of Uzziah." II Kings 15 (30).

Ahaz (Judah) Tenth Syrian Campaign

"In the seventeenth year of Pekah the son of Remaliah, Ahaz the son of Jotham king of Judah began to reign." II Kings 16 (1).

"Then Rezin king of Syria and Pekah son of Remaliah king of Israel came up to Jerusalem to war; and they besieged Ahaz, but could not overcome him." II Kings 16 (5).

"At that time Rezin king of Syria restored Elath to Syria, and drove the Jews from Elath; and the Edomites came to Elath, and dwelt there, unto this day." II Kings 16 (6)

"So Ahaz sent messengers to Tiglath-pileser king of Assyria, saying: 'I am thy servant and thy son; come up, and save me out of the hand of the king of Syria and out of the hand of the king of Israel, who rise up against me'. And Ahaz took the silver and gold that was found in the house of the Lord, and in the treasures of the king's house, and sent it for a present to the king of Assyria. And the king of Assyria hearkened unto him; and the king of Assyria went up against Damascus, and took it, and carried the people of it captive to Kir, and slew Rezin." II Kings 16 (7, 8, 9).

"And king Ahaz went to Damascus to meet Tiglath-pileser king of Assyria . . ." II Kings 16 (10).

"And Ahaz slept with his fathers, and was buried with his fathers in the city of David; and Hezekiah his son reigned in his stead." II Kings 16 (20).

Hoshea (Israel)
Third Assyrian Attack
Exile of the Ten Tribes

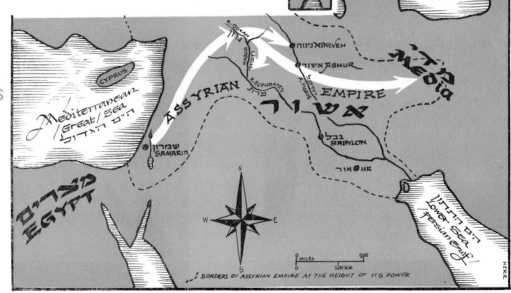

"In the twelfth year of Ahaz king of Judah began Hoshea the son of Elah to reign in Samaria over Israel, and reigned nine years." II Kings 17 (1).
"Against him came up Shalmaneser king of Assyria; and Hoshea became his servant, and brought him presents." II Kings 17 (3).
"And the king of Assyria found conspiracy in Hoshea; for he had sent messengers to So king of Egypt, and offered no present to the king of Assyria, as he had done year by year; therefore the king of Assyria shut him up, and bound him in prison." II Kings 17 (4).
"Then the king of Assyria came up throughout all the land, and went up to Samaria, and besieged it three years." II Kings 17 (5).

"In the ninth year of Hoshea, the king of Assyria took Samaria, and carried Israel away unto Assyria, and placed them in Halah, and in Habor, on the river of Gozan, and in the cities of the Medes." II Kings 17 (6).

"And the king of Assyria brought men from Babylon, and from Cuthah, and from Avva, and from Hamath and Sepharvaim, and placed them in the cities of Samaria instead of the children of Israel; and they possessed Samaria, and dwelt in the cities thereof." II Kings 17 (24).

Hezekiah (Judah)—Fourth Assyrian Attack

"Now it came to pass in the third year of Hoshea son of Elah king of Israel, that Hezekiah the son of Ahaz king of Judah began to reign." II Kings 18 (1).

"And the Lord was with him: whithersoever he went forth he prospered; and he rebelled against the king of Assyria, and served him not." II Kings 18 (7).

"He smote the Philistines unto Gaza and the borders thereof, from the tower of the watchmen to the fortified city." II Kings 18 (8).

"Now in the fourteenth year of king Hezekiah did Sennacherib king of Assyria come up against all the fortified cities of Judah, and took them." II Kings 18 (13).

"And Hezekiah king of Judah sent to the king of Assyria to Lachish, saying: 'I have offended; return from me; that which thou puttest on me will I bear'. And the king of Assyria appointed unto Hezekiah king of Judah three hundred talents of silver and thirty talents of gold." II Kings 18 (14).

"And the king of Assyria sent Tartan and Rab-saris and Rab-shakeh from Lachish to king Hezekiah with a great army unto Jerusalem. And they went up and came to Jerusalem. . . ." II Kings 18 (17). *Note: See also Isaiah* 36.

"So Rab-shakeh returned, and found the king of Assyria warring against Libnah; for he had heard that he was departed from Lachish." II Kings 19 (8).

"And it came to pass that night, that the angel of the Lord went forth, and smote in the camp of the Assyrians . . . So Sennacherib king of Assyria departed, and went and returned, and dwelt at Nineveh." II Kings 19 (35, 36).

Note: Hezekiah was succeeded by Manasseh (see II Kings 20 (21)) and Manasseh was succeeded by Amon. See II Kings 21 (18).

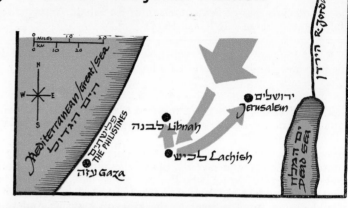

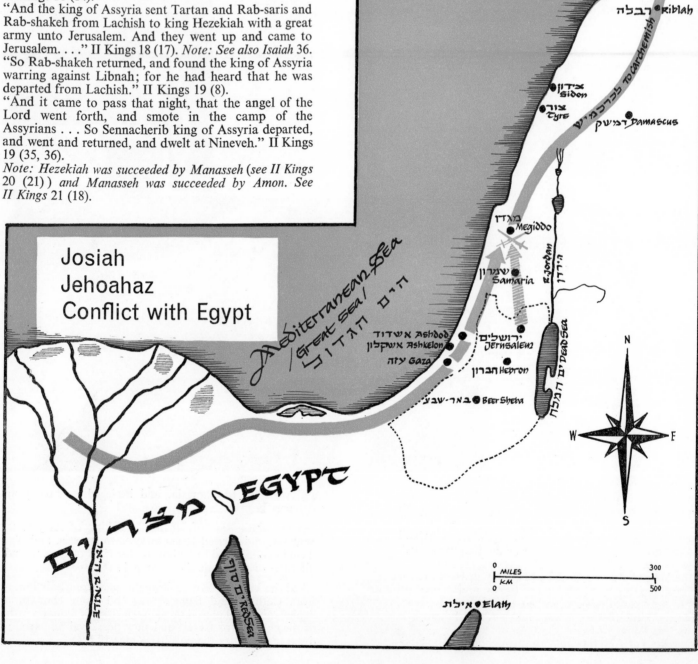

Josiah
Jehoahaz
Conflict with Egypt

"And he (*Amon*) was buried in his sepulchre in the garden of Uzza; and Josiah his son reigned in his stead." II Kings 21 (26).

"Josiah was eight years old when he began to reign; and he reigned thirty and one years in Jerusalem . . ." II Kings 22 (1).

"In his days Pharaoh-necoh king of Egypt went up against the king of Assyria to the river Euphrates; and king Josiah went against him; and he (*Pharaoh*) slew him (*Josiah*) at Megiddo, when he had seen him." II Kings 23 (29).

"And his servants carried him in a chariot dead from Megiddo, and brought him to Jerusalem, and buried him in his own sepulchre. And the people of the land took Jehoahaz the son of Josiah, and anointed him, and made him king in his father's stead." II Kings 23 (30).

"And Pharaoh-necoh put him (*Jehoahaz*) in bands at Riblah in the land of Hamath, that he might not reign in Jerusalem; and put the land to a fine of a hundred talents of silver, and a talent of gold. And Pharaoh-necoh made Eliakim the son of Josiah king in place of Josiah his father, and changed his name to Jehoiakim; but he took Jehoahaz away; and he came to Egypt, and died there." II Kings 23 (33, 34).

Jehoiakim (Judah)—first Babylonian Invasion

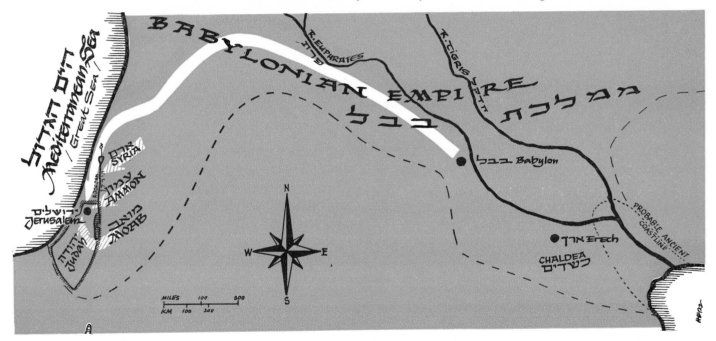

"Jehoiakim was twenty and five years old when he began to reign; and he reigned eleven years in Jerusalem . . ." II Kings 23 (36).

"In his days Nebuchadnezzar king of Babylon came up, and Jehoiakim became his servant three years; then he turned and rebelled against him." II Kings 24 (1).

"And the Lord sent against him bands of the Chaldeans, and bands of the Syrians, and bands of the Moabites, and bands of the children of Ammon, and sent them against Judah to destroy it, according to the word of the Lord, which He spoke by the hand of His servants the prophets." II Kings 24 (2).

"So Jehoiakim slept with his fathers . . ." II Kings 24 (6).

Note: See also the Book of Jeremiah for many references to this period, e.g. Chapters 25–27, 35 and 36.

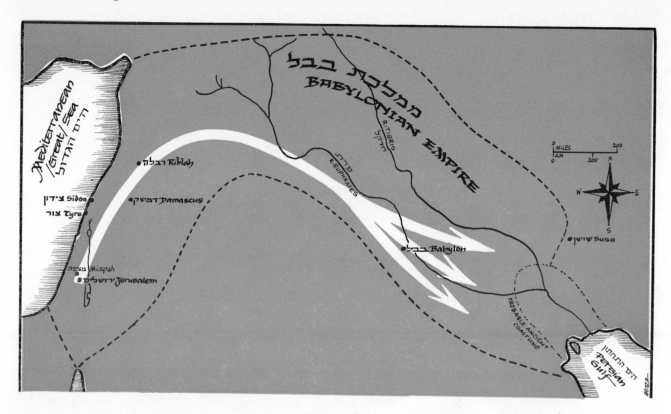

"So Jehoiakim slept with his fathers; and Jehoiachin his son reigned in his stead. And the king of Egypt came not again any more out of his land; for the king of Babylon had taken, from the Brook of Egypt unto the river Euphrates, all that pertained to the king of Egypt." II Kings 24 (6, 7).

"At that time the servants of Nebuchadnezzar king of Babylon came up to Jerusalem, and the city was besieged." II Kings 24 (10).

"And he (*Nebuchadnezzar*) carried away all Jerusalem, and all the princes, and all the mighty men of valour, even ten thousand captives, and all the craftsmen and the smiths; none remained save the poorest sort of the people of the land. And he carried away Jehoiachin to Babylon; and the king's mother, and the king's wives, and his officers, and the chief men of the land, carried he into captivity from Jerusalem to Babylon. And all the men of might, even seven thousand and the craftsmen and the smiths a thousand, all of them strong and apt for war, even them the king of Babylon brought captive to Babylon. And the king of Babylon made Mattaniah his father's brother king in his stead, and changed his name to Zedekiah." II Kings 24 (14–17).

". . . And Zedekiah rebelled against the king of Babylon." II Kings 24 (20).

"And it came to pass in the ninth year of his reign, in the tenth month, in the tenth day of the month, that Nebuchadnezzar king of Babylon came, he and all his army, against Jerusalem, and encamped against it; and they built forts against it round about." II Kings 25 (1).

"Then they took the king, and carried him up unto the king of Babylon to Riblah; and they gave judgement upon him. And they slew the sons of Zedekiah before his eyes, and put out the eyes of Zedekiah, and put him in fetters, and carried him to Babylon." II Kings 25 (6, 7).

"Now in the fifth month, on the seventh day of the month, which was the nineteenth year of king Nebuchadnezzar, king of Babylon, came Nebuzaradan the captain of the guard, a servant of the king of Babylon, unto Jerusalem. And he burnt the house of the Lord, and the king's house; and all the houses of Jerusalem, even every great man's house, burnt he with fire. And all the army of the Chaldeans that were with the captain of the guard, broke down the walls of Jerusalem." II Kings 25 (8–10).

"And the rest of the people that were left in the city, and the fugitives that fell to the king of Babylon, with the remnant of the multitude, did Nebuzaradan the captain of the guard carry away captive." II Kings 25 (11).

Note: See also Jeremiah 52 and II Chronicles 36.

"And as for the people that remained in the land of Judah, whom Nebuchadnezzar king of Babylon had left, even over them he made Gedaliah the son of Ahikam, the son of Shaphan, governor." II Kings 25 (22).

"But it came to pass in the seventh month, that Ishmael the son of Nethaniah, the son of Elishama of the seed royal, came, and ten men with him, and smote Gedaliah, that he died, and the Jews and the Chaldeans that were with him at Mizpah." II Kings 25 (25).

The Persian Empire

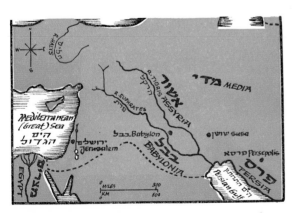

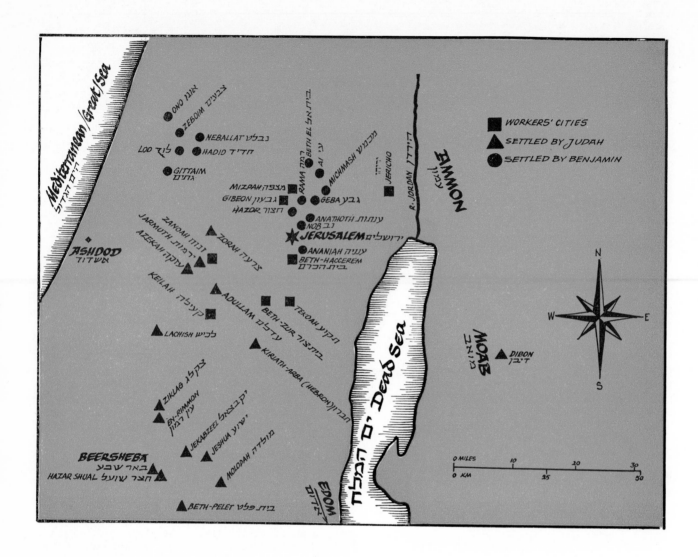

"Now in the first year of Cyrus king of Persia, that the word of the Lord by the mouth of Jeremiah might be accomplished, the Lord stirred up the spirit of Cyrus king of Persia, that he made a proclamation throughout all his kingdom and put it also in writing, saying: 'Thus saith Cyrus king of Persia: All the kingdoms of the earth hath the Lord, the God of heaven, given me; and He hath charged me to build Him a house in Jerusalem, which is in Judah. Whosoever there is among you of all His people—his God be with him—let him go up to Jerusalem, which is in Judah, and build the house of the Lord, the God of Israel, He is the God who is in Jerusalem. And whosoever is left, in any place where he sojourneth, let the men of his place help him with silver, and with gold, and with goods, and with beasts, beside the freewill offering for the house of the God which is in Jerusalem.' " Ezra 1 (1–4).

Note: See also II Chron. 36 (22-23).

"Then rose up the chiefs of fathers of Judah and Benjamin, and the priests, and the Levites, even all whose spirit God had stirred to go up to build the house of the Lord which is in Jerusalem." Ezra 1 (5).

"The whole congregation together was forty and two thousand three hundred and sixty. Beside their men-servants and their maid-servants, of whom there were seven thousand three hundred and thirty seven; and they had two hundred singing men and singing women." Ezra 2 (64, 65).

"And some of the heads of fathers' houses, when they came to the house of the Lord which is in Jerusalem, offered willingly for the house of God to set it up in its place." Ezra 2 (68).

"Now in the second year of their coming unto the house of God at Jerusalem, in the second month, began Zerubbabel the son of Shealtiel, and Jeshua the son of Jozadak, and the rest of their brethren the priests and the Levites, and all they that were come out of the captivity unto Jerusalem; and appointed the Levites, from twenty years old and upward, to have the oversight of the work of the house of the Lord." Ezra 3 (8).

"And the elders of the Jews builded and prospered, through the prophesying of Haggai the prophet and Zechariah the son of Iddo. And they builded and finished it, according to the commandment of the God of Israel, and according to the decree of Cyrus, and Darius, and Artaxerxes king of Persia. And this house was finished on the third day of the month Adar, which was in the sixth year of the reign of Darius the king." Ezra 6 (14, 15).

"Now after these things, in the reign of Artaxerxes king of Persia, Ezra the son of Seraiah, the son of Azariah, the son of Hilkiah, this Ezra went up from Babylon; and he was a ready scribe in the Law of Moses, which the Lord, the God of Israel had given; and the king granted him all his request, according to the hand of the Lord his God upon him. And he came to Jerusalem in the fifth month, which was in the seventh year of the king." Ezra 7 (1, 6, 8).

Note: For details of the towns of Judah whence the workers came, see Nehemiah 3.

"But it came to pass that, when Sanballat, and Tobiah, and the Arabians, and the Ammonites, and the Ashdodites heard that the repairing of the walls of Jerusalem went forward, and that the breaches began to be stopped, then they were very wroth; and they conspired all of them together to come and fight against Jerusalem, and to cause confusion therein." Nehemiah 4 (1, 2). AV:4 (7, 8)

"And it came to pass, when our enemies heard that it was known unto us, and God had brought their counsel to nought, that we returned all of us to the wall, every one unto his work." Nehemiah 4 (9). AV:4 (15)

"They that builded the wall and they that bore burdens laded themselves, every one with one of his hands wrought in the work, and with the other held his weapon. And the builders, every one had his sword girded by his side, and so builded. And he that sounded the horn was by me." Nehemiah 4 (11, 12). AV:4 (17, 18)

Note: For details of the towns, other than Jerusalem, settled by the Jews, see Nehemiah 11 (25–36).

Reuben   Simeon

Judah   Issachar

Zebulun   Benjamin

Dan   Naphtali

Gad   Asher

Ephraim   Manasseh

Kings of Judah and Israel

Saul
David
Solomon

Judah	Israel
approx. 930 B.C.E. Rehoboam	Jeroboam
Abijah	
Asa	
	Nadab
	Baasha
	Elah
	Zimri
	(Tibni)
	Omri
Jehoshaphat	
	Ahab
	Ahaziah
Jehoram	Jehoram
Ahaziah	Jehu
(Queen) Athaliah	
Jehoash	
	Jehoahaz
	Jehoash
Amaziah	
	Jeroboam II
Uzziah	
	Zechariah
	Shallum
	Menahem
Jotham	
	Pekahiah
	Pekah
Ahaz	
	Hoshea
Hezekiah	
Manasseh	**Fall of Samaria**
Amon	(approx. 722 B.C.E.
Josiah	
Jehoahaz	
Jehoiakim	
Jehoiachin	
Zedekiah	

Fall of Jerusalem
Babylonian Exile
(approx. 586 B.C.E.)